CREATIVE MUSIC FUNDAMENTALS

James P. O'Brien

University of Arizona

Prentice-Hall, Inc.   **Englewood Cliffs, New Jersey 07632**

Library of Congress Cataloging in Publication Data

O'BRIEN, JAMES PATRICK.
    Creative music fundamentals.

    Includes index.
    1. Music—Theory, Elementary.   2. Music—Manuals, text-
books, etc.   I. Title.
MT7.02 1984   781   84-1990
ISBN 0-13-190455-8

41,944

Editorial production/supervision
  by Dan Mausner
Page makeup by Meryl Poweski
Manufacturing buyer: Raymond Keating

Printed in the United States of America

10 9 8 7 6 5 4 3 2 1

ISBN 0-13-190455-8 01

PRENTICE-HALL INTERNATIONAL, INC., *London*
PRENTICE-HALL OF AUSTRALIA PTY. LIMITED, *Sydney*
EDITORA PRENTICE-HALL DO BRASIL, LTDA., *Rio de Janeiro*
PRENTICE-HALL CANADA INC., *Toronto*
PRENTICE-HALL OF INDIA PRIVATE LIMITED, *New Delhi*
PRENTICE-HALL OF JAPAN, INC., *Tokyo*
PRENTICE-HALL OF SOUTHEAST ASIA PTE. LTD., *Singapore*
WHITEHALL BOOKS LIMITED, *Wellington, New Zealand*

Contents

Preface

There are many traditional aspects of *Creative Music Fundamentals*. The study of songs is central to the development of musicianship. All 150 songs contained in this volume have been selected from contemporary collections, and cover the major, minor, and pentatonic keys. The student will learn to play instruments, to read and create music, and to listen to selected examples of European masterworks (chosen from the Bowmar Orchestral Library). The approach is adaptable for those who need a basic understanding of music fundamentals, whether elementary education majors, future music majors, or interested students in general.

Unlike many fundamentals texts, this one has close sequencing of musical concepts and skills. These two components of learning are developed simultaneously in each chapter. A skill such as singing, listening, or playing leads to the understanding of a musical concept through immediate and practical application. Most skills and concepts are developed through experience and discovery, not explanation and definition. For precise definitions, a glossary is available. This developmental sequence model is compatible with the learning theories of Bruner and Piaget, and is especially appropriate for elementary education majors.

Each of the fourteen chapters covers a reasonable development of concepts and skills. In an ideal fifteen-week semester, each unit could conceivably cover one week's work. Some instructors may not wish to go as far as the material in the final chapters and can spend more time on earlier chapters as the interests and needs of the students develop. If a short semester requires it, the basic materials can be covered in the first ten or eleven chapters by eliminating one or more of the playing skills.

Creative Music Fundamentals may be used as a total learning package if all skills are compatible with the instructor's objectives. However, it is possible to omit guitar, for example, spend more time on piano throughout, and develop the same concepts. The same is true for the listening examples. If the recorder is used, some songs can be eliminated without sacrificing the inherent sequence. The comprehensive approach may thus provide more material than any one instructor will care to use with all students. But it is there to provide for individual differences of students in those cases where some are required to learn piano but not guitar, or recorder but not autoharp. It also provides alternatives for the instructor semester by semester. It is even possible to proceed through the entire textbook using only singing and then to begin again and proceed with recorder or guitar instruction if this is the course organization.

Music reading and creating become end objectives of each chapter of study. This provides ongoing interest for the learner. One cannot learn literature without a turn at writing poetry, or painting without dabbling with a brush. So it is with music. All can become composers and try to shape sound through the suggestions given. Music making should be fun—after all, we use the phrase "play music," not "work music." This book also provides a model of what music education should be in the elementary classroom.

Each chapter begins with a listing of the concepts which are explored. This provides focus for the learner and instructor. Each chapter concludes with a summarizing list and a self-checking chapter review, which are useful to reinforce the student's learning, or to be used selectively as test questions.

It is well to remember that there is a third domain of learning along with skills and concepts. It is *appreciation*—the valuing of musical pursuits. There is no guarantee that the latter will develop by using this book. There is good indication, however, that one values a subject area if one is competent in it and understands its structure. Mastering skills and concepts generally leads to appreciation—that is the ultimate intent of this book.

J. O'B.

Melody	*folk song ~ pitch*
Rhythm	*beat*
Harmony	*chord*
Form	*unity ~ variety ~ program music ~ absolute music*

Music is organized sound which is intended for people to sing, play, or hear. This suggests that there are special ways to organize as well as to perceive sounds.
Sing:

SHE'LL BE COMIN' ROUND THE MOUNTAIN

		Meter	Key
She'll be Comin' Round the Mountain When she comes, when she comes!	*Phrase 1*	$\frac{2}{4}$	F Major
She'll be Comin' Round the Mountain When she comes, when she comes!	*Phrase 2*		
She'll be Comin' Round the Mountain She'll be Comin' Round the Mountain,	*Phrase 3*		
She'll be Comin' Round the Mountain When she comes, when she comes!	*Phrase 4*		

Most people know this folk song from childhood and can easily sing it because they know how it is organized. A *folk song* is learned by oral tradition; it is not usually written down in formal music notation.

Sing verses that everyone knows to "She'll Be Comin' Round the Mountain."

The tune that everyone sings is an important element in music. It is called the *melody*. Melody is a horizontal element in music consisting of various pitches, the highs and lows of music.

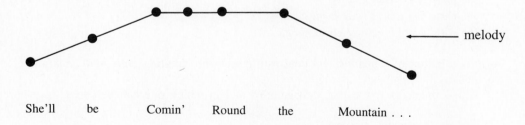

If you tap your toe as you sing, you are responding to the beat, one aspect of an element called *rhythm*.

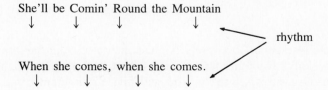

If someone accompanies your singing on the piano, guitar or Autoharp®, a *harmony* is provided. This is a third element of music, consisting of *chords* (several different pitches played simultaneously) that fit well with the melody, that is, they harmonize with the melody. Harmony represents a vertical element of music.

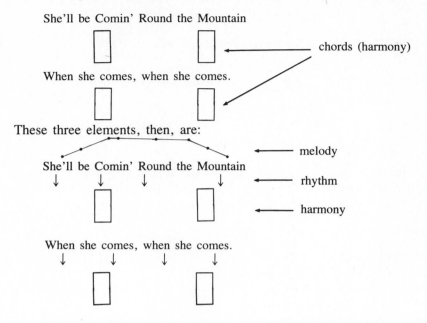

Two additional elements are present as you sing with accompaniment. There is a degree of loudness in all music known as *dynamics*. There are various sound sources, too (instruments and voices). This is known as *timbre* or tone quality. Your voice undoubtedly produces a slightly different timbre than the voice of someone else. A trumpet produces a different timbre from a piano, a synthesizer from a flute, and so forth.

Name several timbres (tone qualities) one often hears in music.

Finally, there is a design in how melody, rhythm, harmony, dynamics, and timbre all work together in the song. Phrase 1 is very similar to phrase 2. Both are very similar to phrase 4. Phrase 3, however, is totally different from the others. *Form* is the interrelationship of all elements:

the parts that repeat exactly
the parts that repeat with slight changes
the parts that are completely different

Form is a matter of repeating and contrasting sections, creating *unity* and *variety* in the music.

Thus, music is sound that is organized and in which one can perceive

melody (horizontal movement)
rhythm (time, including the beat)
harmony (vertical movement)
dynamics (degree of loudness)
timbre (sound source or tone quality)
form (organization and design)

Most music has all of these elements. Only rarely is music heard without harmony and, even rarer, without melody. The other four elements must, to some degree, be present to have music. In most cases, however, you will find all six elements are present.

Sing each of the following songs and consider how they are organized by the six musical elements.

THE CAISSONS GO ROLLING ALONG

	Meter	Key
Over hill, over dale, we have hit the dusty trail And those caissons go rolling along. In and out hear them shout "Counter march and right about," And those caissons go rolling along.	$\frac{2}{4}$	C Major

Then it's Hi! Hi! Hee! in the Field Artillery,
Sound off your numbers loud and strong.
Where'er you go you will always know
That those caissons go rolling along,
And those caissons go rolling along.

POLLY WOLLY DOODLE

	Meter	Key
Oh, I went down south for to see my Sal, Sing Polly Wolly Doodle all the day; Oh, my Salley am a spunky gal, Sing Polly Wolly Doodle all the day. Fare thee well, fare thee well, Fare thee well my fairy Fay, I'm a-gwine to Loosiana for to see my Susie Anna Singing Polly Wolly Doodle all the day.	$\frac{4}{4}$	C Major

HOME ON THE RANGE

	Meter	Key
Oh, give me a home where the buffalo roam, Where the deer and the antelope play; Where seldom is heard a discouraging word And the skies are not cloudy all day.	$\frac{6}{8}$	F Major

Home, home on the range
Where the deer and the antelope play;
Where never is heard a discouraging word
And the skies are not cloudy all day.

STAR-SPANGLED BANNER

	Meter	Key
Oh say, can you see by the dawn's early light What so proudly we hailed at the twilight's last gleaming? Whose broad stripes and bright stars through the perilous fight, O'er the ramparts we watched were so gallantly streaming? And the rockets' red glare, the bombs bursting in air Gave proof through the night that our flag was still there. Oh! say, does that Star-Spangled Banner yet wave O'er the land of the free and the home of the brave?	$\frac{3}{4}$	A♭ Major

This book will lead to a degree of mastery of each element through singing, playing instruments (guitar, recorder, autoharp, piano and various classroom rhythm and percussion instruments), moving and listening to music, reading notation, and creating (organizing) your own sounds.

Listen to

The Moldau by Smetana (1824–1884)
(Bowmar Orchestral Library No. 60)

This is an example of *program music,* music that tells a story or depicts a setting or picture. (*Absolute music,* by contrast, is music that has no extra–musical references.) Smetana describes a river in Czechoslovakia, the Moldau, from its source high in the mountains, to its final and mighty flow to the sea. The piece begins with tiny streams at the river's source, represented by this melody:

The actual river is represented by this melody:

This melody occurs several times as the river continues to build and flow, providing overall unity to the composition.

Variety is provided by the use of other melodies that represent events along the river's banks, such as peasant dancing:

Smetana also depicts a hunter's horn, moonlight on the water, and the passage of the water over treacherous rapids. As you listen, observe how unity and variety are balanced throughout. Observe also how each of the musical elements is employed to create unity and variety.

Self–checking Chapter Review

Find a term in the "word search" below that means the same as or refers to each of the following. (Words may be found in horizontal, vertical or diagonal position, forward or backward.)

1. The vertical element of music
2. Repetition
3. Contrast
4. Music that tells a story
5. The horizontal element of music
6. Design in music
7. A type of song passed by oral tradition
8. Several tones played together
9. Sound source
10. The time element of music
11. Music is organized _____
12. An instrument that produces a specific timbre
13. How many musical elements
14. Another name for melody

```
R  H  A  R  M  O  N  Y  A
H  B  T  U  N  E  T  T  C
Y  D  H  K  T  E  J  I  I
T  E  P  U  I  F  C  N  G
H  M  L  R  M  H  T  U  Y
M  F  A  S  O  U  N  D  D
Q  V  L  R  I  G  N  P  O
R  O  D  T  S  X  R  U  L
V  T  I  M  B  R  E  A  E
Z  W  K  L  O  F  O  R  M
```

2

Melody	double bar
Rhythm	beat notation ~ tie ~ rests
Harmony	D major ~ e minor
Form	duet ~ trio ~ quartet ~ introduction ~ coda

Most music has an underlying beat which is the rhythmic foundation for the composition. Sometimes this beat is audible; at other times, it is measured but inaudible. Beats may thus be heard or felt.

Tap your foot once for each second as you watch the second hand on a watch. This basic tap or beat may be represented in music as: |

Tap this many times: | | | | | | | | | | | | | | etc.

Tap this many times: | | | | | | | |

Clap this many times:

These are all audible beats.

Beats in music may also be silent, in which case a rest is written 𝄾.
    𝄾 𝄾 𝄾 𝄾 means to rest four beats.
    Rest this many times, feeling each silent beat.

Rests must be measured exactly as beats that are sounded.
    Tap the following line, resting one full beat each time you see a 𝄾:

Clap the following:

Snap your fingers to the following:

Tap the above three lines without pausing using the second hand on a watch as your underlying beat.

5

Woodblocks   Drum   Sticks

Photo by Donald Smith,
Slide City, Tucson, Arizona.

Perform as a class following composition using woodblocks, sticks and drums.

| = 60 per minute

Perform as a class composition assigning a different instrument to each line. A line of music enclosed by ‖: :‖ (double bars) is repeated before the next line is performed.

Woodblocks

Sticks

Drums

Write a composition for woodblocks, sticks and drums using double bar repeats and at least twelve beats per line. (Place 3 beats between | |.)

Wood blocks

Sticks

Drums

6

Beats may be made longer by ties. A tie ⌣ means only the first beat is sounded; all others within the tie are measured as inaudible beats.

⌣   sounded once, but held for two

⌣⌣   sounded once, but held for three

Perform as a group the following on woodblocks, sticks and drums.

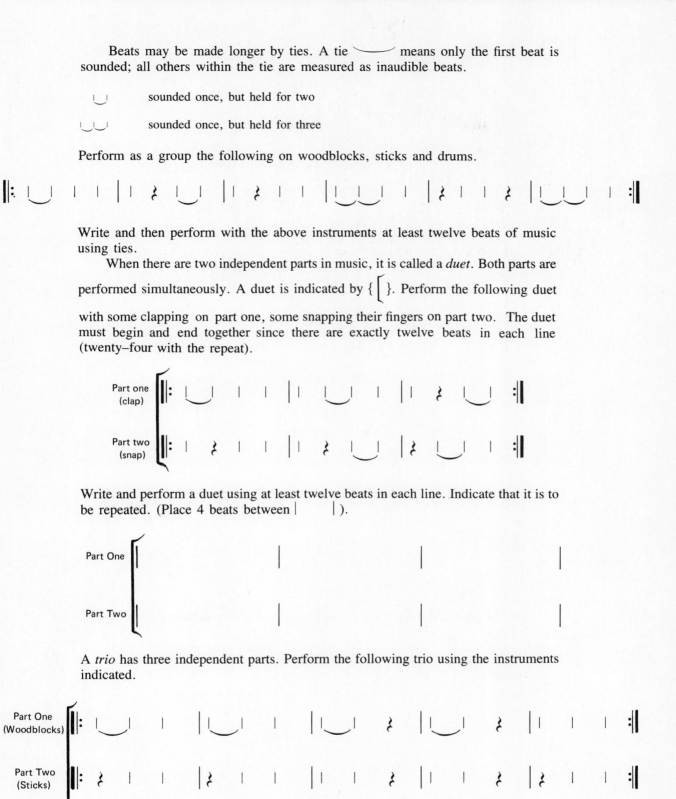

Write and then perform with the above instruments at least twelve beats of music using ties.

When there are two independent parts in music, it is called a *duet*. Both parts are performed simultaneously. A duet is indicated by { [}. Perform the following duet with some clapping on part one, some snapping their fingers on part two. The duet must begin and end together since there are exactly twelve beats in each line (twenty–four with the repeat).

Part one
(clap)

Part two
(snap)

Write and perform a duet using at least twelve beats in each line. Indicate that it is to be repeated. (Place 4 beats between | |).

Part One

Part Two

A *trio* has three independent parts. Perform the following trio using the instruments indicated.

Part One
(Woodblocks)

Part Two
(Sticks)

Part Three
(Drums)

Perform the following trio using the body sounds indicated:

Clap

Patschen*

Tap

* slap thigh

Write and perform a trio that combines body sounds with the rhythm instruments:

Part one

Part two

Part three

Walk to the following lines of music, pausing at each 𝄽 or tie ()

walk   walk   pause   walk   walk   walk   walk   pause

Walk to the following lines of music, changing direction on each new line of music.

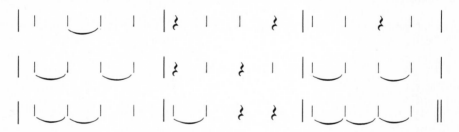

Split the class and walk to the following duet, changing direction on each new line of music.

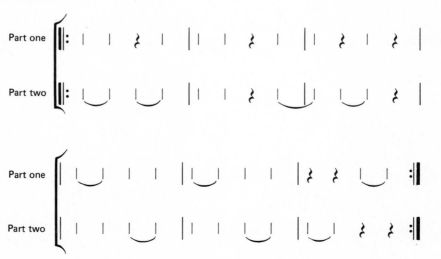

Part one

Part two

Part one

Part two

Write and then perform a composition of at least thirty-two beats, incorporating movement (walking) and instruments or body sounds.
Sing "Are You Sleeping, Brother John?"

Are You Sleeping?

French Round

Are you sleep - ing, Are you sleep - ing, Broth - er John, Broth - er John?
Frè - re Jac - ques, Frè - re Jac - ques, Dor - mez vous, Dor - mez vous?

Morn - ing bells are ring - ing, Morn - ing bells are ring - ing, Ding, dang, dong! Ding, dang, dong!
Son - nez les ma - ti - nes, Son - nez les ma - ti - nes, Din, dan, don! Din, dan, don!

Repeat as you tap the following beat or play on a rhythm instrument.

Accompany the singing with a rhythm instrument on the beat.
Walk to the underlying beat as you sing the melody again.
Perform the following rhythm as you sing the melody again.

Walk to the above rhythm as you sing the song.
Write a sixteen beat rhythm with repeat to perform or move to as you sing "Are You Sleeping?"
An Autoharp is a harmony instrument. Chords are played by pressing down a bar and strumming the string on each beat.

"Autoharp" is a trade name for this instrument. It is also called a Chromaharp by some companies. The Autoharp is usually placed on a table. The chord bars are depressed with the left hand as the right hand crosses over and strums on the long part of the string from bottom to top. Photo by Donald Smith, Slide City, Tucson, Arizona.

9

Find the D major chord button on the Autoharp. Strum four times. | | | |
Accompany the melody on *Are You Sleeping?* using the D major chord.

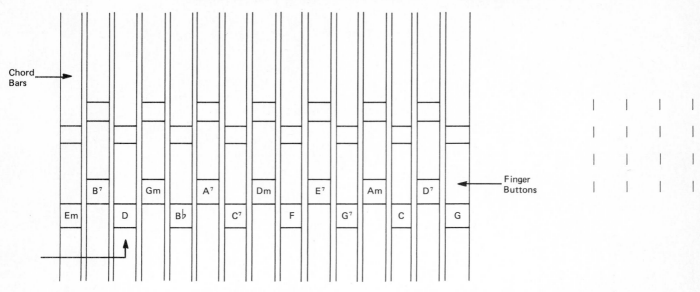

Chords may also be played on the guitar. The left hand fingers the chord on the neck of the guitar while the right hand strums downward.

Photo by Donald Smith, Slide City, Tucson, Arizona.

Strum the D major chord on the guitar. This chord is played as:

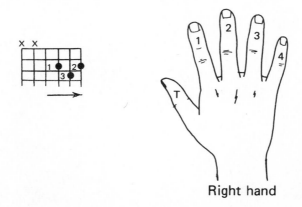

Right hand

10

Do not strum on the strings marked "X".

An *introduction* may precede the singing of a song. A *coda* is the conclusion after the singing ends. Sing and accompany "Are You Sleeping?" with the following rhythms, using the introduction and coda.

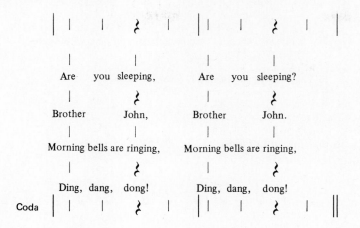

Sing "Hey, Ho! Nobody Home."

Hey, Ho! Nobody Home

From *Guitar in the Classroom*, 1971, Timmerman and Griffith (Dubuque: William C. Brown)

Play and sing *Hey, Ho! Nobody Home* with the guitar e minor chord, adding the introduction and coda as indicated.

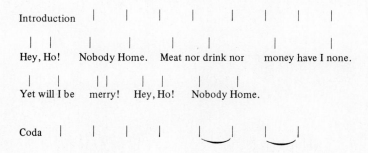

Write your own introduction, accompaniment and coda to "Hey, Ho!" (Use eight beats in both the introduction and coda. Sixteen beats are needed for the accompaniment.) Perform what you have written.

Introduction (8 beats) — — — — — — — —

Hey, Ho! Nobody Home. Meat nor drink nor money have I none.

Yet will I be merry! Hey, Ho! Nobody Home.

Coda (8 beats) — — — — — — — —

In traditional music notation, the beat (|) is often written as a *quarter note*, ♩. Perform the following:

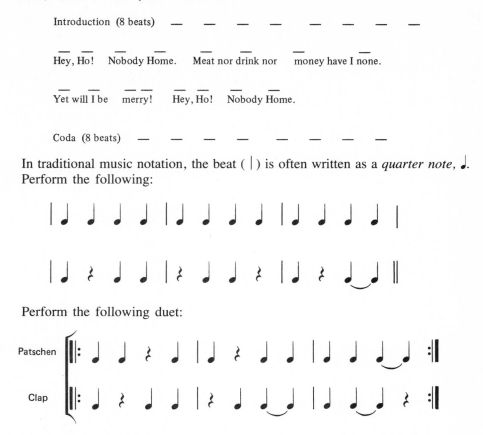

Perform the following duet:

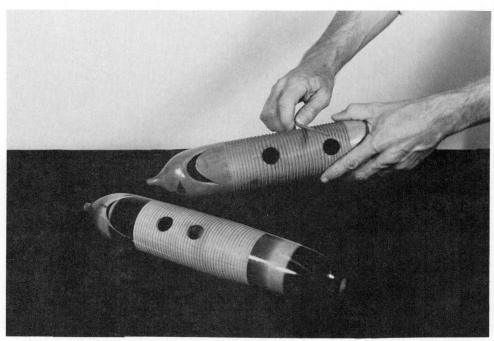

Perform the following *quartet,* a composition for four independent parts, using the guiro, a scraping instrument.

The Guiro

Photo by Donald Smith,
Slide City, Tucson, Arizona.

Write a trio for body sounds or a quartet for the above instruments. Use at least twenty beats in each line.

Listen to

"The March of the Siamese Children" by Rodgers
(Bowmar Orchestral Library No. 54)

Choose one of the following to accompany the recording as you listen. Repeat the pattern until the end of the composition.

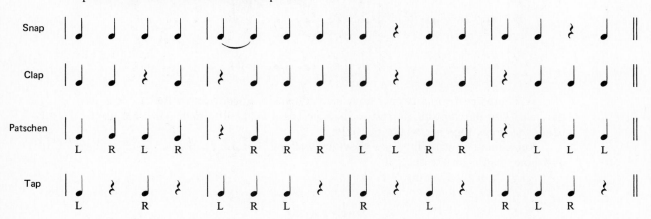

Write and perform a sixteen beat pattern as you...

Listen to

"Stars and Stripes Forever" by Sousa (1854-1932)
(Bowmar Orchestral Library No. 54)

Other notes may be used to write the basic beat. These include the half note ($\flat$), the eighth note ($\flat$), or the dotted quarter note ($\flat$.).

The half note ($\flat$) has an open note head with a stem. The stem may go up ($\flat$) or down ($\flat$). The equivalent half note rest is ━. Perform the following lines on rhythm instruments. The $\flat$ equals one beat.

Write a sixteen beat composition $\flat$ and ━. Indicate it is to be repeated. Perform it as a duet with one written by someone else.

An eighth note has a black note head, a stem as well as a flag. (♪) The stem may go up (♪) or down (♩). The equivalent eighth note rest is ♪. Perform the following rhythm where ♪ equals one beat.

Eighth notes may be joined together with *beams* as ♫. The meaning is the same. ♫ is equal to ♪♪♪.

Rewrite the above exercise, beaming the eighth notes wherever possible when they are not separated by a rest.

A dotted quarter note looks like a regular quarter note except it has a dot beside it. The equivalent rest is ♪. Perform the following rhythm where ♩. equals one beat.

Write and perform a twenty–four beat composition using either the ♩, ♩ or ♩. as the beat. Use the appropriate rest to indicate silent beats. If eighth notes are used, beam the notes together where possible.

Repeat any or all of the lines above by walking. For ♩♩, ♩♩ or ♩. ♩., walk on the first note, pause on the second.

Sing "Lovely Evening."

Lovely Evening

Add the following rhythm as accompaniment. Use the D major chord on the Autoharp and guitar.

The rhythm of the accompaniment, which is the beat in this example, as well as the rhythm of the melody (*melodic rhythm*) work together to create an interesting musical effect.

Sing "Row, Row, Row Your Boat."

Row, Row, Row Your Boat

E. O. Lyte

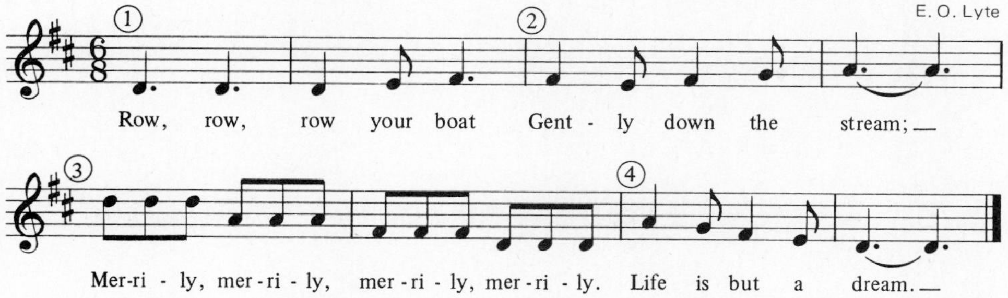

Add the following rhythm as accompaniment. Use the D major chord on the Autoharp and guitar: ♩. ♩., etc.

Again, the beat and the melodic rhythm work together to create the musical effect.

Write and perform an introduction and coda to either of the above accompaniments.

Write and perform a sixteen beat accompaniment as you...

Listen to

the *Colonel Bogey March* by Alford
(Bowmar Orchestral Library No. 54)

Use either the ♩, 𝅗𝅥, ♪ or ♩. (and equivalent rest) as your beat.

Self-checking Chapter Review

Match Column II to Column I

1. _____ Beat
2. _____ Double Bar (with repeat)
3. _____ Tie
4. _____ Duet
5. _____ Trio
6. _____ Patschen
7. _____ Introduction
8. _____ Coda
9. _____ Quarter note
10. _____ Quarter rest
11. _____ Quartet
12. _____ e minor chord
13. _____ Guiro
14. _____ Half note
15. _____ Half rest
16. _____ Eighth note
17. _____ Beamed eighth notes
18. _____ Dotted quarter note
19. _____ Autoharp (Chromaharp)
20. _____ D major chord
21. _____ Eighth rest

A. 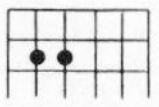
B. Harmony instrument
C. ♪
D. For three parts
E. 𝅗𝅥
F. Before the song
G. ♩
H. For four parts
I. 𝄆 𝄇
J. 𝄽
K. ♩.
L. |
M. Scraped percussion instrument
N. 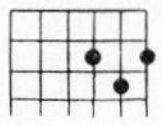
O. For two parts
P. Slap thigh
Q. 𝄼
R. After the song
S. ♫
T. 𝄾
U. ‿

Melody	anacrusis ~ improvisation
Rhythm	tempo terms ~ fermata ~ accelerando ~ ritardando ~ a tempo
Harmony	a minor ~ D major ~ A_7
Form	overture ~ opera ~ aria

In some compositions, beats, whether audible or inaudible, move very quickly. In others, they occur very slowly. The relative speed of the beat is called *tempo*.

Tempos are basically slow, moderate or fast. A moderate tempo has between 80-100 beats per minute, the average pulse of a healthy person. A slow tempo has fewer beats per minute, such as one per second (60 per minute). A fast tempo is one that has more than 100 beats per minute.

Tempo is relative stable in a musical composition, that is, a composition may be in a fast, moderate or slow tempo throughout.

Perform the following duet on *triangles* and *tambourines,* using a slow tempo (about 60 beats per minute.)

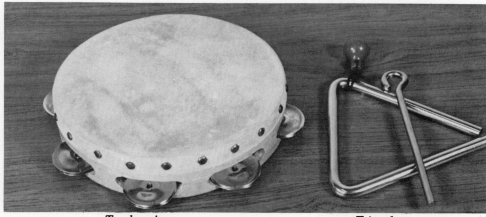

Tambourine   Triangle

Photo by Donald Smith,
Slide City, Tucson, Arizona.

Composers indicate slow tempos in many ways. Most frequently, they write an Italian word that means "slow." Among these are:

Grave (extremely slow)
Largo (very slow)
Adagio (slow)
Andante (walking tempo)

They may also use a *metronome* to indicate the duration of the beats. A metronome may be adjusted to sound as few as 40 beats per minute or as many as 208 beats.

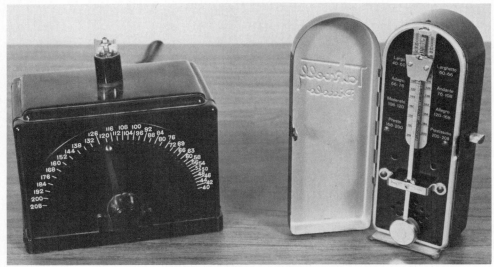

♩ = 80

♪ = 120

♩. = 132 - 136

𝅗𝅥 = 72

Photo by Donald Smith,
Slide City, Tucson, Arizona.

Metronome

The second hand on a watch (or the display on a digital timepiece) can approximate a metronomic marking:

      60 beats = 1 beat per second
    120 beats = 2 beats per second
    180 beats = 3 beats per second

Moderate tempos include:

      Andantino (faster than Andante)
       Moderato (moderately)
         Allegretto (moderately fast)

Fast tempos include:

      Allegro (quick and lively)
       Presto (very fast)
         Prestissimo (extremely fast)

Listen to

    Overture to *The Bat* (*Die Fledermaus*) by Johann Strauss, Jr. (1825–1899)
    (Bowmar Orchestral Library No. 76)

An *overture* is a "curtain raiser" for an *opera*, a dramatic work that is sung, staged, and accompanied by an orchestra. Overtures often present several of the melodies which will later be sung in the Opera. This is true of "The Bat."

Listen for each of the following melodies. What is the tempo where each occurs? How does the composer move from one tempo to the next? What are the tempo markings above each melody?

Strauss' opera is a comedy about a masked ball and social flirtation. The leading man, Dr. Eisenstein, has been called "The Bat" after having been found intoxicated in the street wearing a bat costume. Many beautiful solo songs (*arias*) are presented.

Italian tempo terms do not represent an absolute speed of the beat like a metronomic mark, but they do give a general speed as well as an overall spirit of a composition. Arranged from slowest to fastest, the basic Italian terms are:

[Slow ⟵⟶ Fast]

Grave
  Largo
    Adagio
      Andante
        Andantino
          Moderato
            Allegretto
              Allegro
                Presto
                  Prestissimo

Perform the following rhythms using classroom instruments.

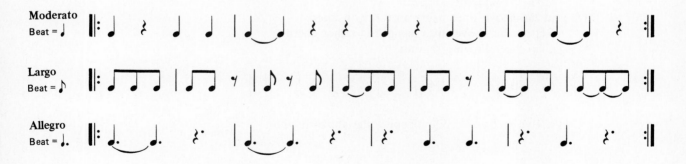

Move to the above rhythms, maintaining the specified tempo.

The tempo of a song may be interrupted by the use of a *fermata* ⌒, a slight hold. Sing "Beside Thy Cradle," observing each ⌒.

Beside Thy Cradle

From Christmas Oratorio,
by Johann Sebastian Bach

Beside_ Thy cra-dle here I stand, O_ Thou that ev - er_ liv - est,

And bring_ Thee with a will-ing hand The_ ver-y gifts Thou_ giv - est.

Ac - cept me; 'tis my mind _ and heart, My soul, my strength, my

ev - 'ry part, That _ Thou from me re - quir - est.

Listen to

Carnival of the Animals by Saint–Saens (1835–1921)
(Bowmar Orchestral Library No. 51)

Which animals are fast? Moderate? Slow? Which is the fastest? Slowest? Which has a tempo that changes? Why?

On the guitar or Autoharp, find the a minor chord.

Strum the a minor chord slowly on the following rhythm.

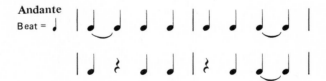

Repeat the above lines using an e minor chord.
Repeat the above lines using a D major chord.
Clap the following rhythm.

Sing "Bye'm Bye" while clapping the above rhythm.

Bye'm Bye

Texas Folksong

Bye'm bye, bye'm bye, Stars shin - ing, shin - ing num - ber one, num - ber

two, num-ber three, num-ber four, num-ber five, Oh my, Bye'm bye, bye'm bye, Oh my! Bye'm bye.

Play the D major chord on the above rhythm while singing "Bye'm Bye."
When a word or two occurs before the main downbeat, as with the word "Bye'm,"
this is referred to as an upbeat or *anacrusis*.

Clap the following rhythm:

E minor and a minor chords are alternated throughout the following composition.
Sing "Wayfaring Stranger," clapping the above rhythm while observing where e minor and a minor chords are to be played.

Wayfaring Stranger

From *Guitar in the Classroom*, 1971. Timmerman and Griffith (Dubuque: William C. Brown)

Divide the class into two groups, assigning half to play the e minor chord, half
the a minor chord where indicated in the music, while everyone sings. ("I'm just a"
is the anacrusis.)

Change chord assignments and repeat the song.

Try playing both chords while singing. If playing the guitar, first practice slowly
changing between the two chords.

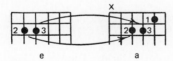

Clap the following rhythm:

Snap to the same rhythm as you sing "Go Tell Aunt Rhodie."

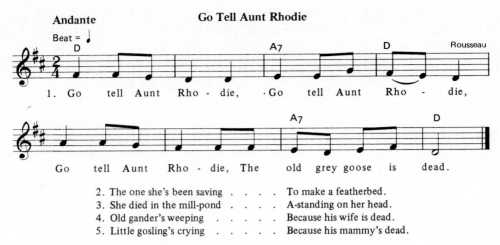

Go Tell Aunt Rhodie

Andante

Rousseau

1. Go tell Aunt Rho - die, Go tell Aunt Rho - die,

Go tell Aunt Rho - die, The old grey goose is dead.

2. The one she's been saving . . . . To make a featherbed.
3. She died in the mill-pond . . . . A-standing on her head.
4. Old gander's weeping . . . . . Because his wife is dead.
5. Little gosling's crying . . . . . Because his mammy's dead.

From *Guitar in the Classroom,* 1971, Timmerman and Griffith (Dubuque: William C. Brown)

Notice that two chords are used in the song, D major and A₇. A₇ is fingered on the guitar:

A₇

Divide the class so half plays D major, half A₇. Sing and play your assigned chords. There is no anacrusis. (Autoharps should be able to play *both* chords.)

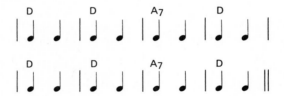

Change chords and repeat.

Try the song playing both chords. Practice slowly changing between the two chords.

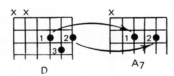

Accompany the following song using the D major and A₇ chords. There is no anacrusis.

Jacob's Ladder

Spiritual

Allegro
Beat =

1. We are climb - ing Ja - cob's lad - der, We are climb-ing Ja - cob's lad - der,

22

We are climb-ing Ja cob's lad-der, sol-diers of the cross.

2. Every round goes higher, higher, etc.
3. Sister, do you love your Jesus? etc.
4. Brother, do your love my Jesus? etc.
5. If you love Him, you must serve Him, etc.
6. We are climbing higher, higher, etc.

From *Guitar in the Classroom,* 1971, Timmerman and Griffith (Dubuque: William C. Brown)

The D major and A₇ chords can also be played on the piano (which is true of all chords). Three tones are used in each chord. The D major chord is found by first locating a group of two black keys.

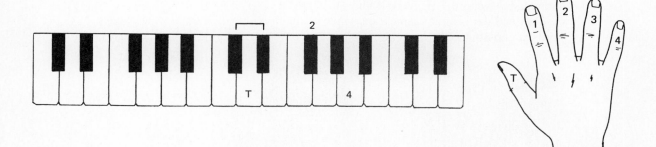

Play the white key between these two black keys with the thumb of your right hand. This tone is called "D." Add the black key marked "2" with the second finger of the right hand. This tone is called F sharp. Add the white key marked "4'''" with the fourth finger of the right hand. This tone is called A. Play all three tones of the D major chord at once. The D major chord consists of three tones: D, F♯ and A.

The tones of the A₇ chord are found by first locating the group of two black keys again.

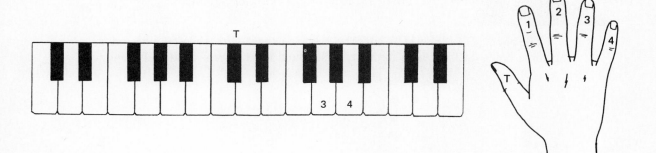

Play the black key marked "T" with the thumb of the right hand. This note is C sharp (C♯). Play the white key marked "3" with the third finger of the right hand. This note is G. Play the white key marked "4" with the fourth finger of the right hand. This note was used in the D major chord, too, and is called A. Play all three tones of the A₇ chord at once. The A₇ chord consists of four tones: C♯, G, A, and E, but E is sometimes omitted, as here, to simplify playing on the piano.

Repeat "Go Tell Aunt Rhody" and "Jacob's Ladder," accompanying on the piano.

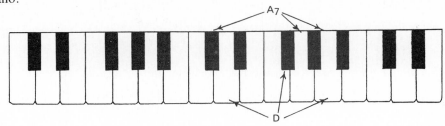

Write a twenty–four beat pattern using the ♩ as the basic beat. Include rests and ties. Begin and end on a D major chord, but indicate where you would like to use e minor and A₇ chords. Play the rhythm on guitar or Autoharp.

Moderato

Beat = ♩

Improvisation means to make up music without notating it. Improvisations are impromptu. Improvise a twenty–four beat pattern using ♩ and ♩ as well as D major, e minor, and A₇ chords. Begin and end on D major.

The recorder is an instrument on which many individual pitches may be played. Chords are possible only when three or more recorders are playing different pitches.

The instrument is placed slightly in the mouth at a 45 degree angle from the body. The left hand is on top, the right hand below with its thumb balancing the instrument. Photo by Donald Smith, Slide City, Tucson, Arizona.

The pitch "G" is played by covering the hole in back with the left thumb and the top three holes on front with the first, second and third fingers of the left hand.

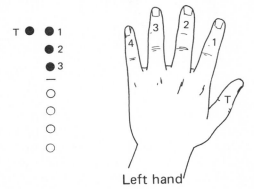

Left hand

Blow gently to produce a pleasant sound, taking care to be certain each hole is completely covered. Let the tongue move against the mouthpiece very slightly to begin and end each note.

24

Play this rhythm on the pitch "G." Tongue each note.

The pitch "A" is played by lifting the third finger, keeping all other holes covered as with "G."

Play the following rhythm on the pitch "A." Tongue each note.

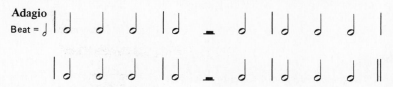

Write a rhythm of at least sixteen beats, using ♪ as the beat, including rests. Play it on the pitch "G." Repeat on "A."

Allegretto
Beat = ♪

The pitch "B" is played by lifting the second finger, keeping all other holes covered as with "A."

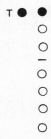

Play the following rhythm on the pitch "B." Tongue each note.

Repeat the above rhythms using the pitch "A," then "G."

Write three lines of rhythm, sixteen beats to the line, using ♩ as the beat. Incorporate ties and rests.

Moderato
Beat = ♩

Line 1

Line 2

Line 3

Play the first line on B, the second on A, and the third on G.

Play this song

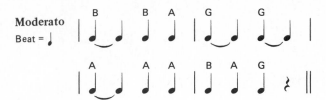

Play this song.

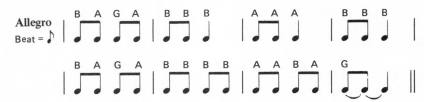

Write a song of at least sixteen beats that begins and ends on G, but which includes changes to A and B throughout. Use the ♩ as the basic beat and include rests and ties. Put words to your song and sing it.   Moderato
Beat = ♩

Listen to

In the Hall of the Mountain King by Grieg (1843–1907)
(Bowmar Orchestral Library No. 59)

What happens to the tempo? The speeding up of the tempo in music is called an *accelerando*.

Listen to

Hungarian Dance No. 5 by Brahms (1833–1897)
(Bowmar Orchestral Library No. 55)

What happens to the tempo? A slowing down of the tempo in music is called a *ritardando*. A return to the original tempo in music after an accelerando or a ritardando is called *a tempo*.

Additional Italian terms referring to tempo and style include:

agitato (with agitation)

animato (with animation and movement)

appassionato (with passion and pathos)

cantabile (in a singing style)

con brio (with spirit)

con moto (with motion)

dolce (sweetly)

espressivo (expressively)

grazioso (with grace)

maestoso (with majesty)

mosso (motion, movement in tempo)

sostenuto (sustained)

The following terms qualify a tempo or style marking:

assai (very) i.e. assai maestoso = very majestically
meno (less) i.e. meno mosso = less motion, slower
molto (much) i.e. molto forte = much loudness
non troppo (not too much) i.e. allegro non troppo = lively but not fast
più (more) i.e. più mosso = more motion, faster
poco (little) i.e. poco a poco accelerando = get faster gradually
sempre (always) i.e. sempre moderato = always in a moderate tempo

Self–checking Chapter Review

Complete the following:

1. the symbol for fermata _____
2. a device for setting tempo _____
3. a term for speeding up _____
4. a term for slowing down _____
5. an operatic solo song _____
6. the a minor chord (put in fingerings)

7. the A_7 chord (put in fingerings)

8–12. the names of these keys

13–15. the names of these pitches

16. to make up music with notating it _____

Which term is the slowest (in each group of three)?

17. presto, largo, moderato
18. adagio, allegro, presto
19. allegretto, grave, allegro
20. andante, moderato, allegro

Match Column II to Column I

21. ___ *cantabile*   A. with agitation
22. ___ *dolce*   B. sweetly
23. ___ *maestoso*   C. with majesty
24. ___ *sostenuto*   D. less
25. ___ *meno*   E. in a singing style
26. ___ *agitato*   F. little
27. ___ *poco*   G. with spirit
28. ___ *sempre*   H. much
29. ___ *molto*   I. sustained
30. ___ *con brio*   J. always

Melody	staff notation ~ treble clef ~ descant ~ key signatures ~ accidentals
Rhythm	accented beat ~ meter signatures ~ measure ~ ostinato
Harmony	G major ~ D_7 ~ C major
Form	first and second endings

Beats are seldom perceived as being equal. In the tick–tock of a mechanical clock, one beat is slightly louder than the other.

The regular grouping of beats results in *accented beats*. The notation of accented beats in traditional music is reflected in the *meter signature*.

When beats are heard as strong–weak, the accent grouping is termed *duple*. Every other beat is thus accented.

strong   weak   strong   weak   strong   weak   *etc.*

Listen to

Marche Militaire by Schubert (1797–1828)
(Bowmar Orchestral Library No. 54)

Notice the strong–weak underlying pulsation. (Is this program or absolute music? Why?)

If the basic beat = ♩, the symbol $\frac{2}{4}$ is often used. This means a strong–weak grouping with the quarter note receiving the beat.

Groups of notes are separated into measures of equal duration, each divided by a *bar line*. Measures are also called *bars* for short.

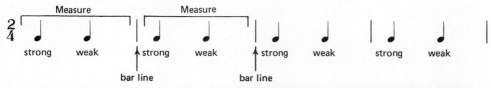

Measure   Measure

$\frac{2}{4}$ strong   weak   strong   weak   strong   weak   strong   weak

bar line   bar line

Bongo drum   *Claves*   *Photo by Donald Smith, Slide City, Tucson, Arizona.*

Play as a group the following $\frac{2}{4}$ rhythm on the bongo drum, conga drum, and claves.

The conga drum will play the strong first beat of each measure, the claves the weak second beat. The first beat will be played on the larger bongo head, the second beat on the smaller head.

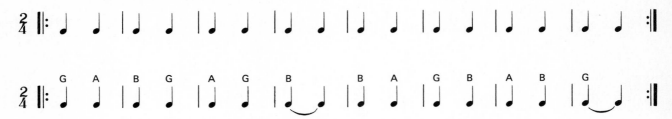

Add the following part on recorders to the above line.

Play this line:

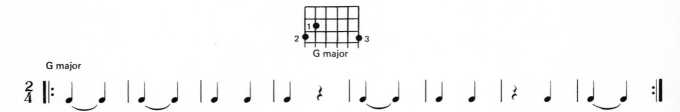

Improvise a short melody on recorder in $\frac{2}{4}$ using the same three pitches. Add the following part on Autoharp and guitar to the rhythm and recorder lines.

Write a twelve measure composition in $\frac{2}{4}$, using rests and ties, with three distinct parts (trio), played by:

    Part 1—conga drums, bongo drum, and claves
    Part 2—recorders, using G, A, and B (Begin and end on G.)
    Part 3—guitars and Autoharps using G major and e minor chords (Begin and end on G major.)

Be certain each part has the same number of beats.
    Improvise a twelve measure composition in a similar manner.
    Part 1—$\frac{2}{4}$
    Part 2—$\frac{2}{4}$
    Part 3—$\frac{2}{4}$

Improvise a twelve measure composition in a similar manner.

Listen to the following compositions in duple meter.

    "Dance of the Sugar Plum Fairy"
    "Trepak"
    "Arabian Dance"
    From the *Nutcracker Suite* by Tchaikovsky (1840–1893)
    (Bowmar Orchestral Library No. 58)

How do the tempos of each vary? Does this affect the duple meter? Are accelerando and ritardando used? How does this affect the music?

Sing "Billy Boy," which is in $\frac{2}{4}$ meter. Notice the $\frac{2}{4}$ is written only on the top line of the music.

Billy Boy

3. Did she give you a chair, Billy Boy, Billy Boy?
   Yes, she gave me a chair, but there was no bottom there,

4. Can she make a cherry pie, Billy Boy, Billy Boy?
   She can make a cherry pie, quick as a cat can wink her eye,

5. Can she cook and can she spin, Billy Boy, Billy Boy?
   She can cook and she can spin, she can do most anything,

6. How old is she, Billy Boy, Billy Boy?
   Three times six and four times seven, twenty-eight and eleven,

Accompany your singing with this rhythmic *ostinato* (repeated pattern). An anacrusis occurs on "Oh."

$\frac{2}{4}$ ♩ ♩ | *etc.*

stamp clap

How many times will you repeat this? (That is, how many measures are there, not counting the anacrusis?)

Accompany your singing on the piano, Autoharp, or guitar with the following rhythm, using D major and A₇ chords.

Add a four measure introduction and a four measure coda (in D major) and repeat.

Two new pitches on the recorder are D and C sharp (C♯).

D is fingered as: C♯ is fingered as:

Practice playing between D and C# on the recorder, adding B, A, and G.

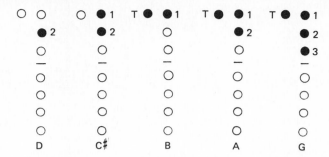

Add the following lines on the recorder while some sing "Billy Boy" and others accompany on rhythm and harmony instruments.

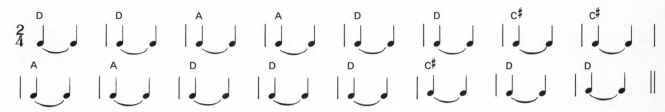

Pitches are notated in music on a *staff*. Each line and space on a staff represents a distinct pitch. The pitch G is identified by the *treble (G) clef,* the circle of which shows the line G.

The other pitches we have learned on the recorder are higher than G. They occur above the line G in this order.

The treble staff has five lines and four spaces, G traditionally being the second line from the bottom.

The *descant* (second melody) to "Billy Boy" above looks like this in staff notation. Repeat it, following the notation on the staff.

Write a six bar melody in $\frac{2}{4}$ for the five recorder tones: G, A, B, C♯, and D. Begin and end on G. (Use rests and ties.)

Improvise eighteen beats of $\frac{2}{4}$ using these five recorder pitches. Begin and end on G. Sing "The Bus Song."

The Bus Song

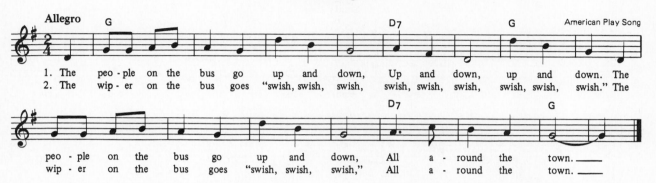

American Play Song

1. The peo-ple on the bus go up and down, Up and down, up and down. The
2. The wip-er on the bus goes "swish, swish, swish, swish, swish, swish, swish, swish, swish." The

peo-ple on the bus go up and down, All a-round the town.____
wip-er on the bus goes "swish, swish, swish," All a-round the town.____

3. The brake on the bus goes, "Roomp, roomp, roomp!" etc.
4. The money in the bus goes, "Clink, clink, clink," etc.
5. The wheels on the bus go 'round and 'round, etc.
6. The driver on the bus says, "Watch your step!" etc.
7. The horn on the bus goes, "Toot, toot, toot," etc.

From *Singing on Our Way* of OUR SINGING WORLD series, ©Copyright, 1959, 1957, 1949 by Ginn and Company (Xerox Corporation). Used with Permission

Accompany on the guitar or Autoharp using G major and D₇ chords.

D₇

anacrusis

The people on the bus . . . . . .

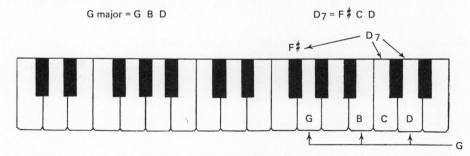

These chords can also be played on the piano.

G major = G B D   D₇ = F♯ C D

Practice the following descant on the recorder and add it to "The Bus Song."

Add the accompaniment on the piano, Autoharp, and guitar as some sing.

Sing "Sandy Land."

Sandy Land

Allegretto

Oklahoma Play–Party Song

1. Make my liv-in' in sand-y land, Make my liv-in' in sand-y land,

Make my liv-in' in sand-y land, La-dies, fare you well.

2. One big tractor to plow the land,
   Ladies fare you well.

3. Raise sweet potatoes in sandy land,
   Ladies, fare you well.

4. Dig sweet potatoes in sandy land,
   Ladies, fare you well.

5. Trucking sweet potatoes into town,
   Ladies, fare you well.

Reprinted by permission of Curtis Brown, Ltd. ©1937, 1963 by B. A. Botkin

Add the following harmonic accompaniment on piano, Autoharp, and guitar. (There is no anacrusis.)

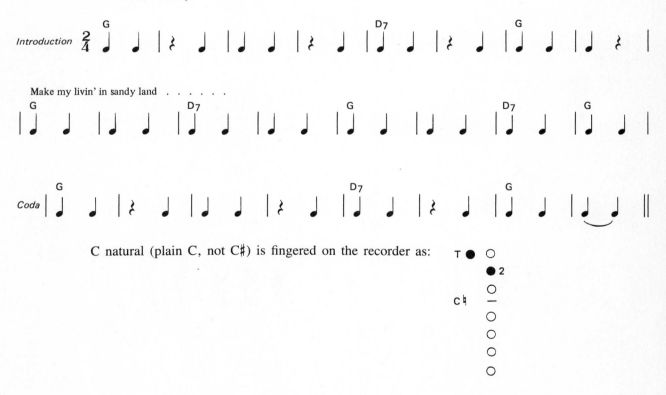

C natural (plain C, not C♯) is fingered on the recorder as:

Add this descant to "Sandy Land" on the recorder.

Write an eight measure melody in $\frac{2}{4}$ for the recorder using G, A, B, C, C♯, and D.
You may use ties and rests. Begin and end your melody on G.

Write a rhythmic accompaniment for rhythm instruments and perform it with the melody.

Improvise a rhythmic accompaniment with the same instruments.

Duple time in music may be seen in meters other than $\frac{2}{4}$. Both $\frac{2}{2}$ and $\frac{2}{8}$ are commonly found. Even $\frac{6}{8}$, known as a *compound meter,* is usually considered duple time.

In $\frac{2}{2}$ time, each measure has two counts, a strong and a weak one, with the ♩ receiving the beat. A $\frac{2}{2}$ meter is often written with a ¢ (*alla breve*) meter signature instead of $\frac{2}{2}$.

Sing "A Bell Noel" which is written in ¢ meter. Note the double bars, which are used for repeating the first and second verses. The ending is marked "1,2." After singing the third verse, this ending is skipped and the one marked "3" is used.

A Bell Noel

3. Bells, ring peace for all today,
Ring ev'rywhere the story!
Ring, the Prince of Peace this day
Was born in manger lowly!

Add the following harmonic accompaniment to "A Bell Noel." There is no anacrusis.

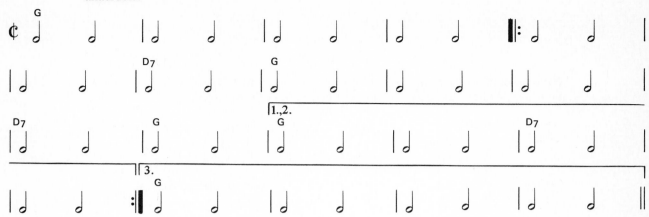

$\frac{2}{8}$ meter also means two beats per measure. In this case, however, the ♪ receives the beat.

Sing "Scotland's Burning."

Scotland's Burning

Add the following descant on the recorder to "Scotland's Burning."

Sing the descant on "loo" while others sing the main melody.

$\frac{6}{8}$ is also duple meter with a strong and a weak beat in each measure. The ♪ does not receive the beat in $\frac{6}{8}$ but rather the ♩. Often, $\frac{6}{8}$ is written as $\frac{2}{\cdot}$, which reflects its true function. $\frac{6}{8}$ is a compound meter, so called because its numerator does not reflect the actual number of beats in a measure nor its denominator the actual note counted as the basic beat. The *true* accented beats can be found by dividing the 6 by 3 (6 ÷ 3 = 2 = duple time.)

Sing "Row, Row, Row your Boat."

Row, Row, Row Your Boat

Accompany with rhythm instruments. There is no anacrusis.

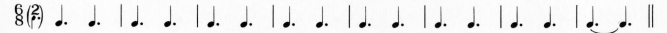

Listen to

"On The Trail" from the *Grand Canyon Suite* by Ferde Grofe (1892–   )
(Bowmar Orchestral Library No. 61)

This is an example of program music depicting a ride on burros into the Grand Canyon. Some parts are in $\frac{6}{8}$, others in $\mathvarnothing$.

Sing "We're All Together Again."

We're All Together Again

Scout Song

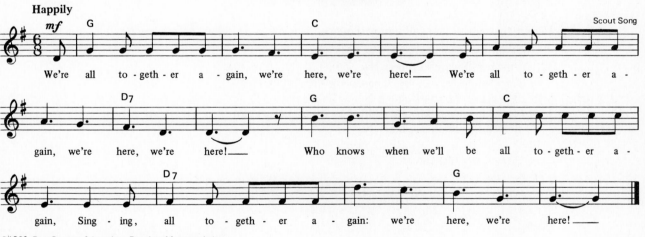

Happily
mf

We're all to-geth-er a-gain, we're here, we're here!___ We're all to-geth-er a-
gain, we're here, we're here!___ Who knows when we'll be all to-geth-er a-
gain, Sing - ing, all to-geth-er a - gain: we're here, we're here!___

Accompany with harmony instruments. The C major chord is new.

The C Major chord is new

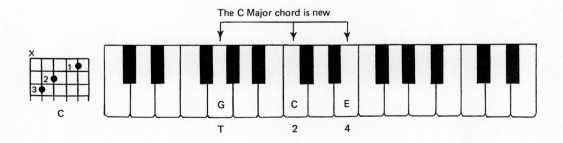

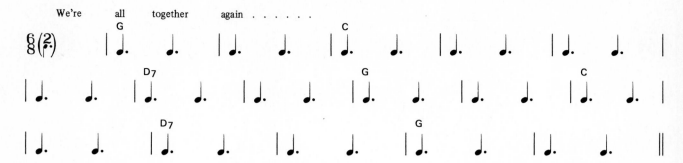

When accented beats are heard in a strong–weak–weak pattern, triple time results.

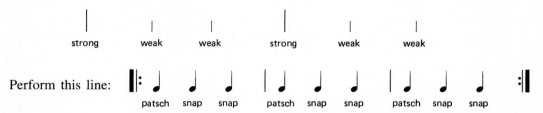

Listen to

Skater's Waltzes by Waldteufel (1837–1915)
(Bowmar Orchestral Library No. 55)

Notice the strong–weak–weak underlying pattern. How are unity and variety achieved?

Triple time is reflected in $\frac{3}{4}$, $\frac{3}{2}$, $\frac{3}{8}$ and $\frac{9}{8}$ meters in which the ♩, 𝅗𝅥, ♪ and ♩. receive the basic beat, respectively.

Listen to each of the following. Each is in triple time. How do the tempos vary?

Grand Waltz by Lecocq (1832–1918)
(Bowmar Orchestral Library No. 56)
Waltz of the Flowers by Tchaikovsky (1840–1893)
(Bowmar Orchestral Library No. 58)
Jesu, Joy of Man's Desiring by J.S. Bach (1685–1750)
(Bowmar Orchestral Library No. 62)

Sing "Join into the Game."

Join Into the Game

Words and music
by Paul Campbell

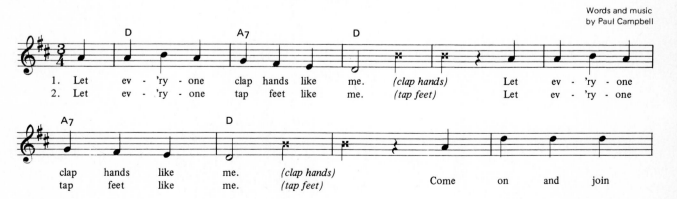

in - to the game;____ You'll find that it's al - ways the same. *(clap hands)*

3. Let ev'ryone nod heads like me. *(nod heads)*
   Let ev'ryone nod heads like me.
   Come on and join into the game;
   You'll find that it's always the same.

4. Let ev'ryone pat knees like me. *(pat knees)*
   Let ev'ryone pat knees like me.
   Come on and join into the game;
   You'll find that it's always the same.

Add the following rhythmic ostinato, using drums on the strong first beat, maracas on the weak second and third beat. ("Let" = anacrusis)

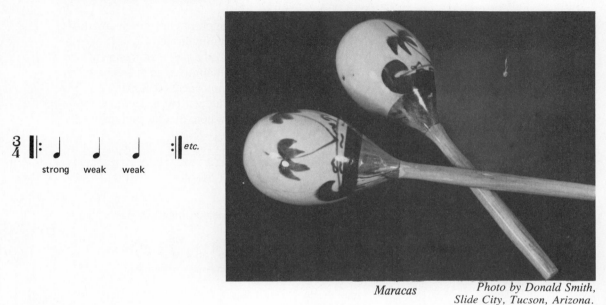

Maracas   *Photo by Donald Smith,*
Slide City, Tucson, Arizona.

Add the following harmonic accompaniment, playing one chord per measure on the strong first beat.

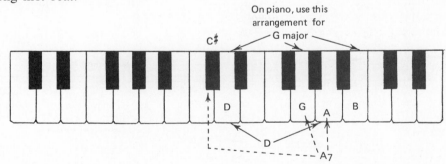

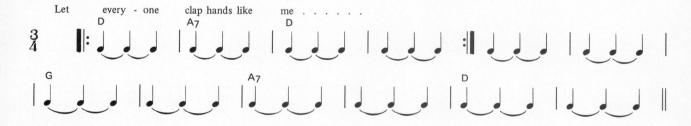

Add the following recorder ostinato to "Join into the Game."

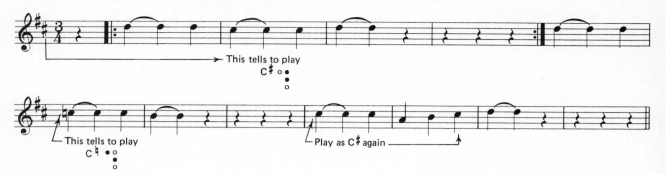

→ This tells to play C# o •
  :
  o

└ This tells to play C♮ • o
  :
  o

└ Play as C# again ───────

A *key signature* at the beginning of a song tells which pitches are sharped (♯, raised a half step) or flatted (♭, lowered a half step.) In "Join into the Game", all F's (top staff line) and C's (second space from top) are played sharp (♯). A change of one of these within the song is called an *accidental*. The C♮ (natural) is an accidental. An accidental applies for *one measure* only since the bar line cancels it (unless it is renewed in the next measure). Accidentals may include a natural (to cancel a sharp or flat note in the key signature) or a sharp (♯) or flat (♭) to a note that has not originally been affected by the key signature.

Play as B♮   Play as F♮   Play as C♯

Sing "The Man on the Flying Trapeze." The $\frac{3}{8}$ meter means there are three counts per measure with the ♪ receiving the count.

*(♪♪ or ♫ = ♪)

two 16th notes = one 8th note

The Man on the Flying Trapeze

American Circus Song

He floats through the air with the great-est of ease, That dar-ing young man on the fly-ing tra-peze; His ac-tions are grace-ful, all girls doth he please; He has sto-len my true love a way. ───

Accompany the song on guitar, Autoharp, or piano. ("He" = anacrusis)

He floats through the air with the . . . . . .

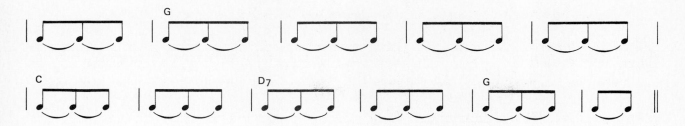

Write a descant for "The Man on the Flying Trapeze," using these notes in place of the chords. Use ♪, ties and rests.

G major = G B D
C major = G and C
D₇ = A,C,D

Are there any sections in which the chord progression repeats? If so, you may repeat this section of the descant.

$\frac{3}{2}$ meter means three beats in a measure with a ♩ receiving each beat. $\frac{9}{8}$ ($\frac{3}{\text{♩.}}$)like $\frac{6}{8}$ is a compound meter with ♩. receiving the beat, three to the measure.

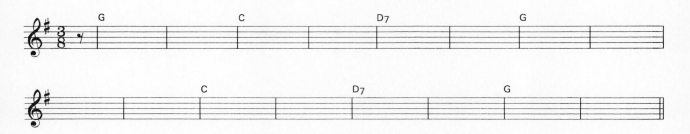

Quadruple meter is four beats to a measure—strong–weak–weak–weak. Often the third beat also receives a slight emphasis—STRONG–weak–strong–weak (although not as strong as the first beat). It is therefore difficult to tell, when listening, whether it is quadruple or duple.

$\frac{4}{4}$ is the most common example of quadruple meter. It is often indicated by ₵, which means *common meter*.

Perform this line:

stamp clap patsch clap   stamp clap patsch clap   stamp clap patsch clap

Listen to each of the following in quadruple meter.

Royal March of the Lion by Saint–Saens (1835–1921)
(Bowmar Orchestral Library No. 51)
March of the Dwarfs by Grieg (1843–1907)
(Bowmar Orchestral Library No. 52)

How does the tempo differ between selections? Why are these examples of program music?

Sing "The Upward Trail." Which note, according to the key signature, is sharp?

The Upward Trail

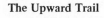

From *Guitar in the Classroom,* 1971, Timmerman and Griffith (Dubuque: William C. Brown)

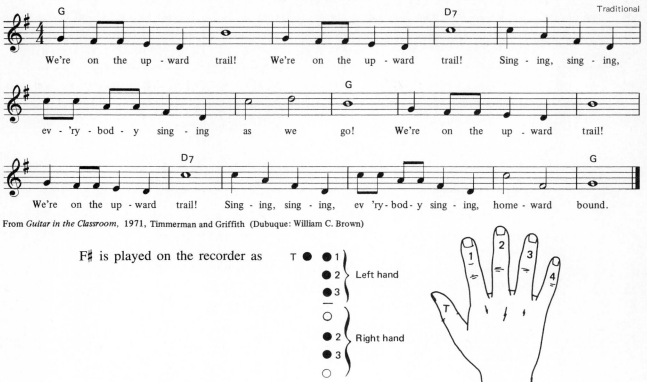

F♯ is played on the recorder as

Practice playing these tones on the recorder.

Improvise a short melody in $\frac{4}{4}$ using these tones. Begin and end on G.

Now add this descant to "The Upward Trail."

Add this accompaniment on harmony instruments. There is no anacrusis.

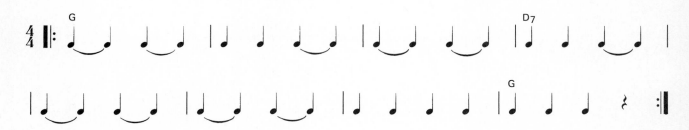

Now write a descant for "The Upward Trail," using these tones in place of the chords. You may write eight measures which repeat, as in the above example. Include ♩, ties, and rests.

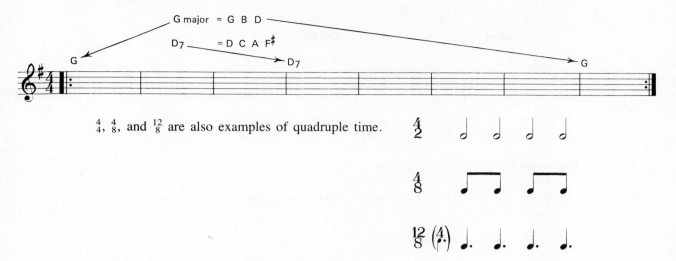

$\frac{4}{4}$, $\frac{4}{8}$, and $\frac{12}{8}$ are also examples of quadruple time.

Listen to each of the following. Which are duple? triple? quadruple?

Minuet by Mozart (1756–1791)
(Bowmar Orchestral Library No. 53)
Triumphal March by Verdi (1813–1901)
(Bowmar Orchestral Library No. 62)
Gypsy Rondo by Haydn (1732–1809)
(Bowmar Orchestral Library No. 63)
Sleeping Beauty Waltz by Tchaikovsky (1840–1893)
(Bowmar Orchestral Library No. 67)

Congo drum

Photo by Donald Smith, Slide City, Tucson, Arizona.

Practice each of these lines. Play on classroom percussion. Play on select recorder tones or guitar/Autoharp/piano chords where appropriate.

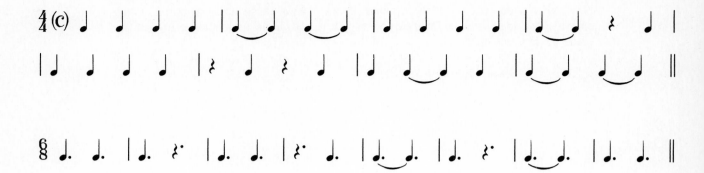

Self-checking Chapter Review

Each of the following note groups represents the basic beat in a given meter. Place the correct meter signature in front of each grouping.

1. ♩ ♩
2. ♫
3. ♩ ♩ ♩ ♩
4. ♩ ♩ ♩
5. ♩. ♩. ♩.

6. ♩. ♩.
7. ♩ ♩
8. ♩ ♩ ♩ ♩
9. ♫ ♫
10. ♩. ♩. ♩. ♩.

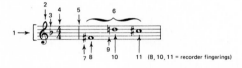

Match these to the numbers given above.

12. [guitar chord diagram]
13. [guitar chord diagram]
14. [guitar chord diagram]
15. descant
16. common time
17. alla breve

A. _____ sharp
B. _____ staff
C. _____ natural
D. _____ C major
E. _____ 𝄴
F. _____ treble clef
G. _____ measure
H. _____ meter signature
I. _____ G major
J. _____ ₵
K. _____ second melody
L. _____ D₇

M. _____ bar line
N. _____ flat

O. _____ [recorder fingering]
P. _____ [recorder fingering]
Q. _____ [recorder fingering]

Melody	leger line ~ conjunct ~ disjunct ~ keynote ~ slur
Rhythm	even pattern ~ dot ~ accent
Harmony	C major ~ G major ~ F major
Form	canon ~ round ~ verse ~ refrain ~ D.C. al Fine ~ D.S. al Fine

Even patterns in rhythm are those that move *with* the pulse or are *evenly divided* over the pulse.

In $\frac{4}{4}$, the pulse is ♩ ♩ ♩ ♩.

All of the following are even patterns.

Write several additional even patterns in $\frac{4}{4}$, using ♩, ♩, ♫ or equivalent rests.

Practice walking to ♩ ♩ ♩ ♩ as you clap one of your even patterns. Improvise several rhythmic lines simultaneously over a steady pulse, using body sounds and rhythm instruments.

A proportion of note values can be established in $\frac{4}{4}$. When ♩ = 1 beat, all the following even combinations are equivalent.

In turn, the half note (♩) = ♩ ♩ and the whole note (o) = ♩ ♩ or ♩ ♩ ♩ ♩. Thus, a proportion in $\frac{4}{4}$ is

whole note		4 counts	(equivalent rest)
half note		2 counts	
quarter note		1 count	
eighth note		½ count	
sixteenth note		¼ count	

Play line one of *Canon* on the recorder. All patterns are even. Two new recorder fingerings are needed.

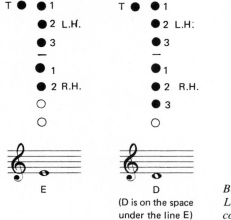

E
(D is on the space under the line E)
D

Blow very gently on these tones. Less breath is needed on the recorder for lower tones.

Canon has a one beat anacrusis. An anacrusis is borrowed from the final measure of a song, which, in this case, has three beats. To begin this piece, count 1–2–3 and play on the 4th beat.

Part 2 is identical to part 1 except that it begins a measure later. Play as a group lines 1 and 2 together as written. A *canon* is a composition with more than one part but in which all parts share the same melody (although each begins it at a different time.)

Canon

Thomas Tallis (1505–1585)

Sing "For Health and Strength," which is also a canon (or *round*) in all even patterns. Notice the anacrusis is one beat. The final measure has only three beats as a result. A dotted half note (♩.) = the value of a regular half note (♩) plus the value of the next smaller note (♩) added together.

3 counts = ♩ ♩ = ♩..
How much is a 𝅝· if ♩ = 1 beat? Hint: 𝅝♩ = ?
Note the lowest note in this song is C (middle C). Since it is below the D space, a line must be added each time it is used. This added line is called a leger line.

For Health and Strength

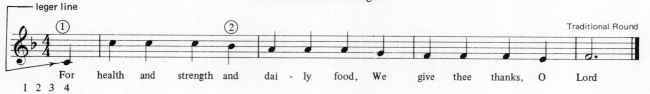

"Puffer Billies" is in $\frac{4}{4}$ and all patterns are even. Count each of the following.

Now tap the pulse with your feet as you clap the melodic rhythm of "Puffer Billies." Observe the repeat.

Puffer Billies

From THIS IS MUSIC FOR TODAY, Book 4 by Sur et al. Copyright ©1971 by Allyn and Bacon, Inc. Used by permission.

47

Sing "Puffer Billies." What is the lowest pitch? Where is it placed? Why? Add these ostinatos on the suggested instruments as you sing.

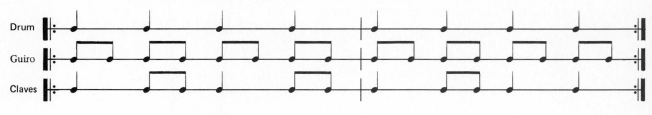

Add this descant on recorders. A new note is needed.

Even patterns in $\frac{2}{4}$, where the pulse is ♩ ♩, are very similar to those in $\frac{4}{4}$. The whole note and dotted half note are not used as such since a measure may contain only two beats.

In "Clocks and Watches" all patterns are even. Count each of the following.

Practice walking to the pulse ♩ ♩ as you clap or play each of the above even patterns.
Sing "Clocks and Watches."

Clocks and Watches

German–American
Liederbuch (1865)

Big clocks tick so slow-ly, tick, tock, tick tock, Lit-tle clocks tick fast-er, tick tock, tick tock, tick tock, tick tock,

Watch-es on your wrist tick fast-er, tic-ke toc-ke, tic-ke toc-ke, tic-ke toc-ke, tick.

> is a musical symbol for *accent*. Accent the notes where > is written by playing each slightly louder. How many different pitches are used in this song?

"Clocks and Watches" can be played on the song bells, resonator bells, step bells, and the piano.

48

Photo by Donald Smith, Slide City, Tucson, Arizona.

Song bells   Resonator bells   Step bells

Try it on all of these instruments. Accompany with a C chord on the guitar and Autoharp.

Write at least three even patterns as ostinatos to be used on rhythm instruments as you perform the above. Add a four measure introduction and coda as well.

Improvise a melody on the above instruments using even patterns with the same pitches. Begin and end on either low or high C.

"This Old Man" has six even patterns. Write them here and practice counting each.

Sing "This Old Man."

This Old Man

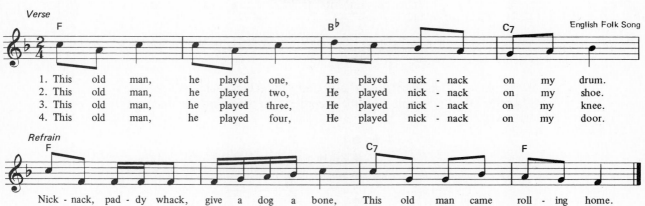

1. This old man, he played one, He played nick - nack on my drum.
2. This old man, he played two, He played nick - nack on my shoe.
3. This old man, he played three, He played nick - nack on my knee.
4. This old man, he played four, He played nick - nack on my door.

Nick - nack, pad - dy whack, give a dog a bone, This old man came roll - ing home.

5. This old man, he played five,
   He played nick-nack on my hive.

6. This old man, he played six,
   He played nick-nack on my sticks.

7. This old man, he played sev'n,
   He played nick-nack 'til elev'n.

8. This old man, he played eight,
   He played nick-nack on my plate.

9. This old man, he played nine,
   He played nick-nack on my spine.

10. This old man, he played ten,
    He played nick-nack on my hen.

A refrain is a chorus which is repeated after the verse each time. Refrains sometimes begin a song too.

What is new in the key signature? The flat (♭) on the line B means each B must be played a half step lower. On the recorder, B♭ is:

Play the following descant to "This Old Man."

Pitches in a melody can move in stepwise motion as in bars three and four of the song. This is called *conjunct* motion. Pitches may also jump or skip as in bars one and two. This is called *disjunct* motion. Where else in the song can you find conjunct motion? Disjunct motion? Where in the descant?

Improvise a short melody on recorder using conjunct motion. Do the same with disjunct motion.

Listen to

"Sleeping Beauty Waltz" by Tchaikovsky (1840–1893)
(Bowmar Orchestral Library No. 67)

There are two main melodies.

Which is conjunct? Disjunct? Listen especially for these qualities.

Play "St. Paul's Steeple" on the recorder. The fingering for middle C is:

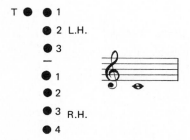

Notice that all notes are natural, there are no sharps or flats. Is there an anacrusis? How many beats are in it? What is the meter? Where is conjunct motion? Disjunct?

St. Paul's Steeple

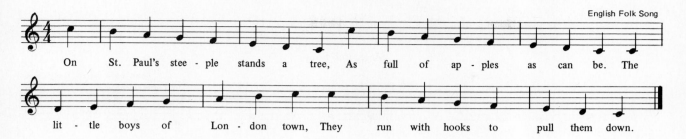

On St. Paul's stee - ple stands a tree, As full of ap - ples as can be. The
lit - tle boys of Lon - don town, They run with hooks to pull them down.

A song with no sharps or flats in its key signature is usually in the key of *C major*. It may begin and end on the pitch C. Is this true for this song? C is thus the *keynote* for this song.

Keynote

Accompany "St. Paul's Steeple" with a C major chord on piano, Autoharp, or guitar, using one of these even patterns.

Add a pitch ostinato on the piano, bells, or recorder as you sing.

Use this as an introduction and coda.

Make up additional even patterns for harmonic accompaniment or as a pitch ostinato using the pitch C.

Play the entire melody on the piano or bells.

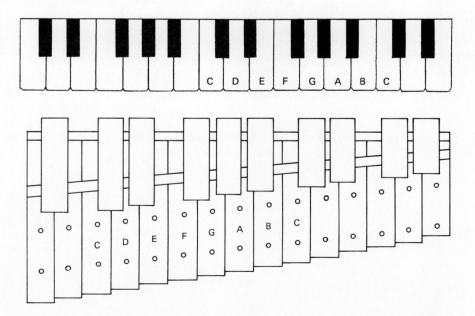

51

Sing and play each of the following songs, observing each of these points:

What is the keynote?
Is there conjunct motion? disjunct motion?
Are there any even patterns?
Is there an anacrusis? How many beats does it have?

Magic Bell Song

Add words to this song. Make the last word of both lines rhyme.

See the Little Ducklings

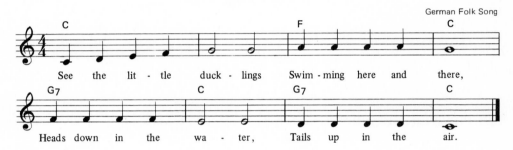

See the lit - tle duck - lings Swim - ming here and there,

Heads down in the wa - ter, Tails up in the air.

Jim Along, Josie

Hey, Jim a - long, Jim a - long, Jo - sie, Hey, Jim a - long, Jim a - long, Joe!

Hey, Jim a - long, Jim a - long, Jo - sie, Hey, Jim a - long, Jim a - long, Joe!

Face to the cen - ter, Hands on your knees, Clap three times and turn a - round, please!
This tells you to *repeat* the first two lines

A song with one sharp (♯) in its key signature is usually in the key of *G major*. This means each F is played as F♯ and that G is the keynote.

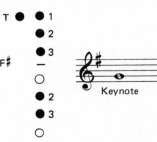

Play and sing each of the following, observing each of these points:

What is the keynote?

Is there conjunct motion? disjunct motion?

Are there any even patterns?

Is there an anacrusis? How many beats does it have?

Good King Wenceslas

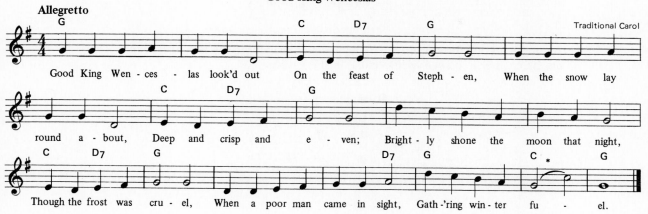

* ♩♪ is a slur. Tongue only the first note. It looks like a tie but is drawn between notes with different pitch names.

Noël

Old MacDonald Had a Farm

Melody

Theme from *First Symphony*
Johannes Brahms (1833–1897)

A song with one flat (♭) in its key signature is usually in the key of *F major*. This means each B is played as B♭ and F is the keynote.

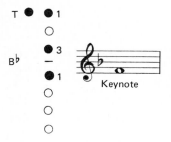

Play and sing each of the following songs, observing each of these points:

What is the keynote?

Is there conjunct motion? Disjunct motion?

Are there any even patterns?

Is there an anacrusis? How many beats does it have?

Au Clair de la Lune

French Folk Melody

Add words to "Au Clair de la Lune." (Note the first line repeats.)

Eins, Zwei, Drei

German Folk Song

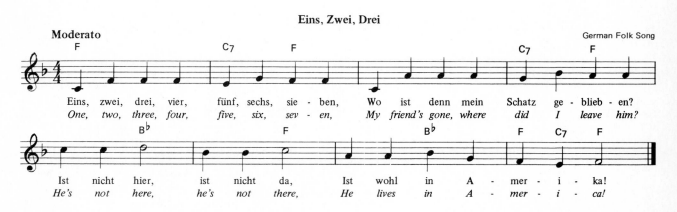

Eins, zwei, drei, vier, fünf, sechs, sie - ben, Wo ist denn mein Schatz ge - blieb - en?
One, two, three, four, five, six, sev - en, My friend's gone, where did I leave him?

Ist nicht hier, ist nicht da, Ist wohl in A - mer - i - ka!
He's not here, he's not there, He lives in A - mer - i - ca!

54

Six Little Ducks

2. Down to the river they would go,
   Wibble, wobble, wibble, wobble,
   to and fro. *(refrain)*

3. Home from the river they would come,
   Wibble, wobble, wibble, wobble,
   ho hum hum. *(refrain)*

Notice the verse–refrain structure in this song.

In considering the above songs in C major, G major, and F major,

Does the song *always* end on the keynote?
Does the song *always* begin on the keynote?
How does the presence of an anacrusis affect the beginning pitch?

Even patterns in $\frac{3}{4}$, where the pulse is ♩ ♩ ♩, are similar to those in $\frac{4}{4}$ and $\frac{2}{4}$. The dotted half note is frequently used. All of the following are typical even patterns in $\frac{3}{4}$ meter.

Improvise a rhythm line in $\frac{3}{4}$ using several of these patterns with body sounds and rhythm instruments.

Find the three even patterns in "Niño Querido." Clap and count each one.

Niño Querido

55

What is the keynote? How is B played?
    Play "Niño Querido" on the recorder.

Accompany on the Autoharp, guitar, or piano. Use one of the following patterns for each measure or write your own even pattern in ¾ for accompaniment.

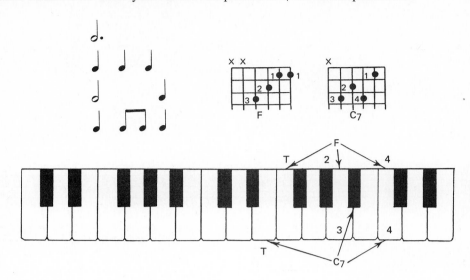

What is the keynote of "Come Rowing With Me"?

Come Rowing With Me

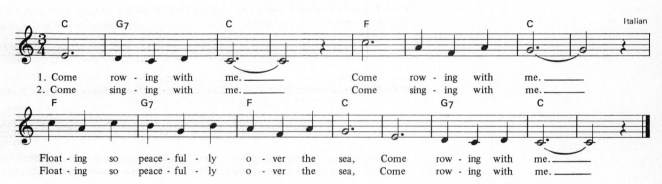

Where is there conjunct motion? Disjunct? Is there an anacrusis? Which lines are identical? How many counts does ♩.│♩ represent?

Play "Come Rowing With Me" on the recorder. How are all Fs and Bs played?

Accompany on harmony instruments, using one of the following even patterns for each measure (or one you write yourself).

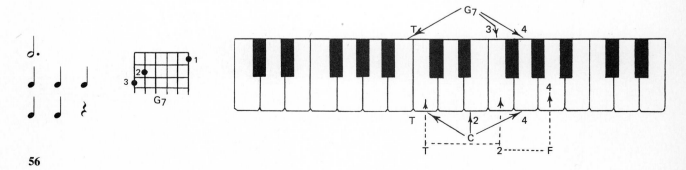

Write a descant for bells or recorder, using even patterns and these chordal tones where appropriate. (Write your descant in predominantly disjunct motion.)

C major = C E G   F major = F A C   G₇ = G B D F

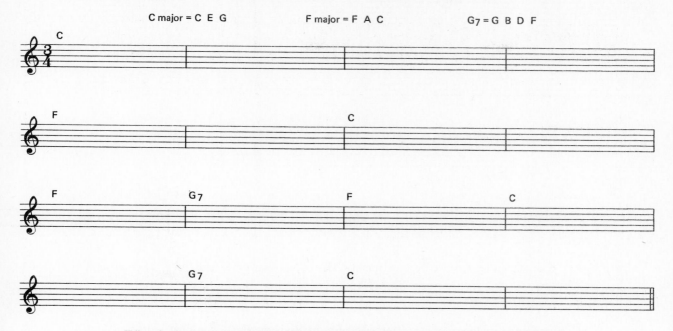

What is the keynote of "East Side, West Side"? How are all Fs played? Where are the ties? Where are the slurs? Play it on the recorder.

East Side, West Side

Charles B. Lawler

James W. Blake

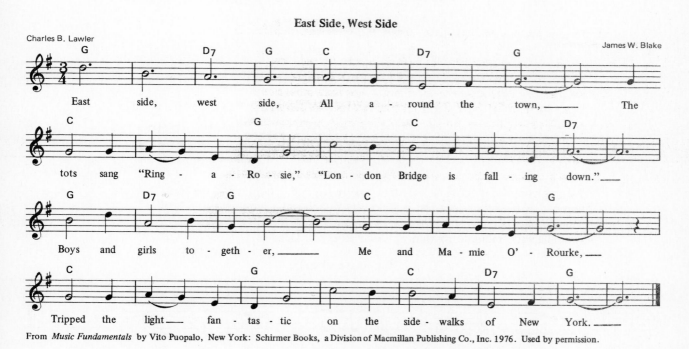

East side, west side, All a - round the town, ____ The

tots sang "Ring - a - Ro - sie," "Lon - don Bridge is fall - ing down." ____

Boys and girls to - geth - er, ____ Me and Ma - mie O' - Rourke, ____

Tripped the light ____ fan - tas - tic on the side - walks of New York. ____

Sing and accompany the song on harmony instruments.

Write a descant using even patterns and these chordal tones where appropriate. (Write your descant in predominantly conjunct motion.)

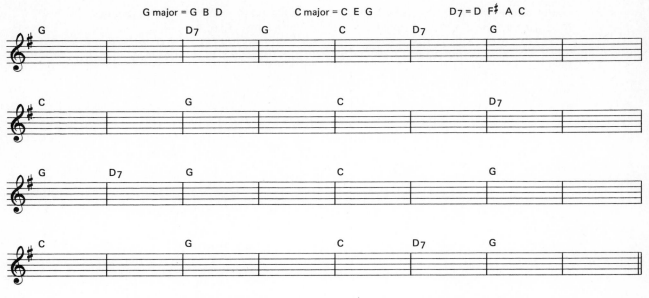

$\frac{6}{8}$ meter is *compound* duple meter. The ♩. receives the beat in $\frac{6}{8}$, two to a measure.

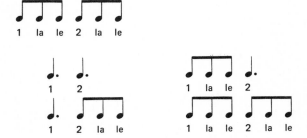

Unlike simple meters ($\frac{2}{4}$, $\frac{3}{4}$, $\frac{4}{4}$, $\frac{2}{2}$, etc.) where the division above the beat is in twos, the division in $\frac{6}{8}$ is in threes. This is counted as:

Even patterns in $\frac{6}{8}$ include:

All compound meters ($\frac{6}{8}$, $\frac{9}{8}$, $\frac{12}{8}$, etc.) have a triple division above the beat. The true number of beats per measure is found by dividing the numerator by 3. Thus, $6 \div 3 = 2$ beats per measure.

Clap the melodic rhythm of "Old Roger is Dead."

Old Roger is Dead

1. Old Rog - er is dead, he is gone to his grave; Ho hum, gone to his grave.
2. Three ap - ple trees grew way up o - ver his head; Ho hum, o - ver his head.
3. The ap - ples were ripe and were read - y to drop; Ho hum, read - y to drop.

4. There came an east wind, 'twas a-blowing them off;
   Ho hum, blowing them off.

5. There came an old woman a-picking them up;
   Ho hum, picking them up.

6. Old Roger jumped up and he gave her a knock;
   Ho hum, gave her a knock.

7. Which made the old woman go hippity hop;
   Ho hum, hippity hop.

Play the melody on the recorder. Sing and accompany with C and G₇ chords on a
♩. ♩. pattern.

Duple, triple, and quadruple time may be conducted with hand patterns which
show the arrangements of beats into strong and weak. Duple time is conducted as:

Practice this pattern.

Conduct a duple pattern with your right hand as you patschen on your left thigh
with these rhythms:

Make up sixteen additional measures of $\frac{2}{4}$ even patterns. Perform these in the above
manner.

Improvise sixteen measures as you conduct.

Patschen the melodic rhythm (rhythm of the words) of "Beautiful Apples" as you
conduct a duple pattern. (*D.C. al Fine* at the end of the song means *da capo al Fine*—
return to the "head" or beginning of the song and repeat until you come to the finish
or *fine* (end of fourth line). *D.S.* (*Dal segno*) is similar to D.C. but means to repeat
from the sign (segno 𝄋) instead of the beginning.

Beautiful Apples

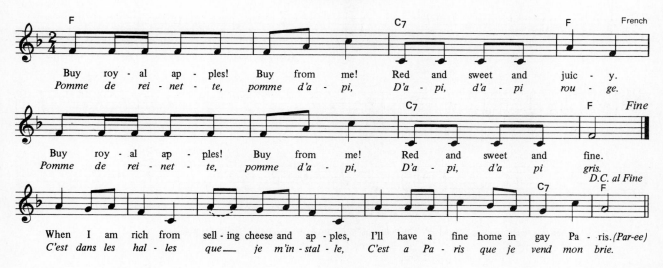

59

Sing "Beautiful Apples" as you conduct. Where do the pitches stay the same? Where is there conjunct motion? Disjunct motion?

Accompany your singing with the F and C$_7$ chords on harmony instruments (Note: The same conducting pattern is used for compound duple meter such as $\frac{6}{8}$).

Triple time is conducted as:

Practice this pattern.

Conduct a triple pattern with your right hand as you patchen on your left thigh with these rhythms.

Create sixteen additional measures of $\frac{3}{4}$ even patterns. Perform these in the above manner.

Improvise sixteen measures as you conduct.

Patschen the melodic rhythm of "Chiapanecas" as you conduct.

Chiapanecas

1. Ay, Chia - pa - ne - cas, ay, ay! (clap, clap) Ay, Chia - pa -
ne - cas, ay, ay! (clap, clap) Ay, Chia - pa - ne - cas, ay,
ay! (clap, clap) Ay, Chia - pa - ne - cas, ay, ay! (clap, clap)

Sing and conduct and accompany on harmony instruments. What is the keynote? How are Bs played? (Note: The same conducting pattern is also used for a compound triple meter such as $\frac{9}{8}$.)

Quadruple time is conducted as:

Practice this pattern

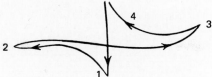

Conduct a quadruple pattern with your right hand as you patschen on your left thigh with these rhythms:

Conductors of musical groups usually use their right hand for beating the time patterns. (The mirror image is suitable for those who are left-handed.) The free hand is used to provide other musical cues—starts, stops, holds, and dynamics. Usually the larger the pattern, the louder the sound.

Create sixteen additional measures of $\frac{4}{4}$ even patterns. Perform these in the above manner.

Improvise sixteen measures as you conduct the $\frac{4}{4}$ pattern.

Patschen the melodic rhythm of "Sleep, Baby, Sleep" as you conduct.

Sleep, Baby, Sleep!
Schlaf, Kindchen, Schlaf!

German Cradle Song

1. Sleep, ba - by, sleep! Thy fa - ther guards the sheep, Thy
Schlaf, Kind - chen, Schlaf!

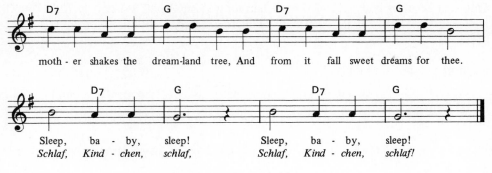

mother shakes the dream-land tree, And from it fall sweet dreams for thee.

Sleep,   ba - by,   sleep!   Sleep,   ba - by,   sleep!
Schlaf,   Kind - chen,   schlaf,   Schlaf,   Kind - chen,   schlaf!

    2. Sleep, baby, sleep!
       The big stars are the sheep;
       The wee stars are the lambs, I guess,
       The fair moon is the shepherdess.
       Sleep, baby, sleep! Sleep, baby, sleep!

Play on the recorder. What is the keynote? How is F played? Sing and accompany yourself on a harmony instrument.

(Note: This conducting pattern is also used for compound quadruple meter such as $\frac{12}{8}$.)

Practice each of these lines. Play on classroom percussion. Play on select recorder tones or guitar/Autoharp/piano chords where appropriate.

62

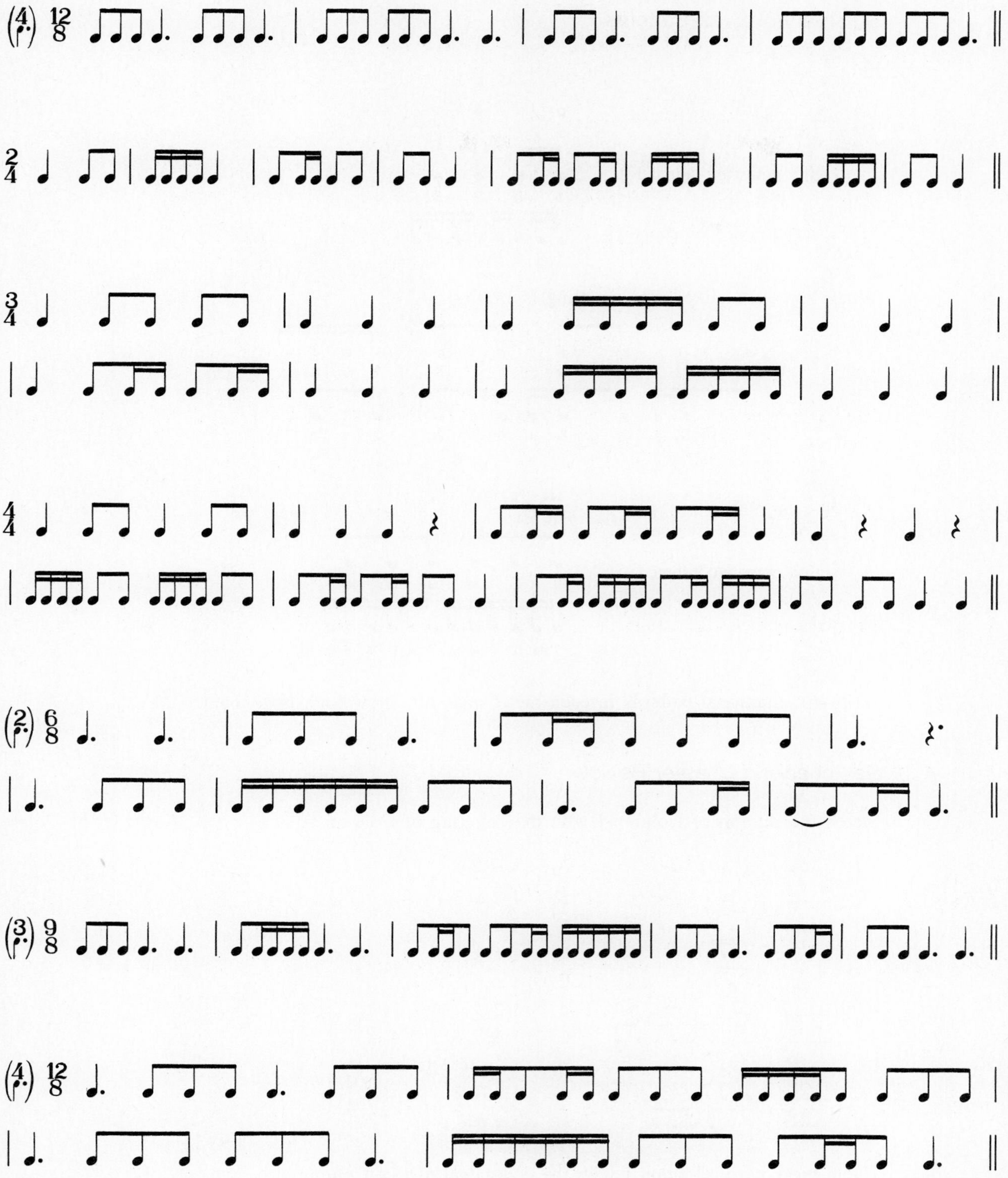

Summary of Even Patterns

In $\frac{2}{4}$, $\frac{3}{4}$, and $\frac{4}{4}$

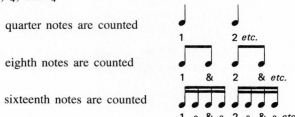

quarter notes are counted

eighth notes are counted

sixteenth notes are counted

When notes are mixed, the counting is similar.

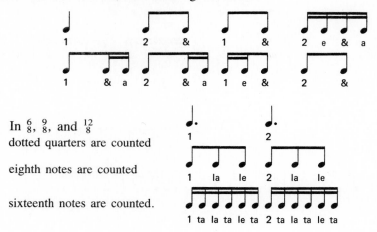

In $\frac{6}{8}$, $\frac{9}{8}$, and $\frac{12}{8}$

dotted quarters are counted

eighth notes are counted

sixteenth notes are counted.

Write six additional patterns in each meter and show how each is counted.

Self-checking Chapter Review

Match the rhythm of Column I with the counting of Column II

1. _____ ♩ ♩ ♩ ♩   A.   1 & 2 3 4
2. _____ ♩ ♫ ♩ ♩   B.   1 2 & 3 4
3. _____ ♫ ♩ ♩   C.   1 2 3 4
4. _____ ♬ ♩ ♩   D.   1 e &
5. _____ ♩ ♫   E.   1 & a
6. _____ ♫.   F.   1 2 3
7. _____ ♫ ♫ ♫ ♫   G.   1 & 2 & 3 & 4 &
8. _____ ♩ ♫ ♩   H.   1 1a 1e 2 1a 1e
9. _____ ♩ ♩ ♩   I.   1 2 & 3
10. _____ ♫ ♩ ♫ ♩   J.   1 e &a

Match the note of Column I with the equivalent rest of Column II.

11. _____ 𝅝   K.   𝄿
12. _____ 𝅗𝅥   L.   𝄼
13. _____ ♩   M.   𝄽
14. _____ ♪   N.   𝄾
15. _____ ♬   O.   𝄻

Match Column II to Column I

(These are recorder fingers except for 5 & 7)

A. B. C. D. E. F.

1. ＿＿＿
2. ＿＿＿
3. ＿＿＿
4. ＿＿＿ SEE ABOVE
5. ＿＿＿
6. ＿＿＿
7. ＿＿＿
8. ＿＿＿
9. ＿＿＿ F major
10. ＿＿＿ C₇
11. ＿＿＿ G₇
12. ＿＿＿
13. ＿＿＿
14. ＿＿＿
15. ＿＿＿ D.S.
16. ＿＿＿ conjunct
17. ＿＿＿ disjunct
18. ＿＿＿ D.C. al fine
19. ＿＿＿ canon
20. ＿＿＿ anacrusis
21. ＿＿＿ ostinato
22. ＿＿＿
23. ＿＿＿
24. ＿＿＿
25. ＿＿＿

G. quadruple time
H. 𝅝ᐧ
I.
J. Go to head of music and repeat to "the end"
K. duple time
L. 𝅗𝅥ᐧ
M. 𝄋
N. slur
O. round
P. skipwise
Q. 𝅘𝅥ᐧ
R. leger line
S. upbeat
T. 𝅘𝅥𝅮ᐧ
U.
V. stepwise
W. repeated pattern
X.
Y. triple time

Melody   *tonic tone ~ dominant tone ~ interval ~ sequence ~ motive*
Rhythm   *uneven patterns*
Harmony   *root*

Music would not continue to have rhythmic interest if every pattern in the melody moved evenly against the pulse. *Uneven* rhythm patterns, in which there is a long-short division of the melodic rhythm over the beat, provide such rhythmic interest.

    Even patterns move against the pulse evenly.

    Uneven patterns, however, move against the beat in a long-short division.

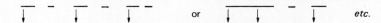

To experience an uneven pattern, first clap on 1-2-3 while saying "1 and 2 and 3 and."

| clap 1 | & | clap 2 | & | clap 3 | & |

Now clap on the "one," "and" of 2, and "three."

| clap 1 | & 2 | clap & | clap 3 | & |

The first pattern is even.

    1 & 2 & 3 &

The second pattern is *uneven*.

    1 & 2 & 3 &

A dot is a frequent signal in simple meters that an uneven pattern will result.

When ♩ = 1 beat, the dot, which lengthens a note's value by one half, adds the value of a ♪, as shown below.
    Thus

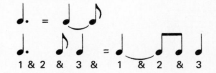

1 & 2 & 3 &   1 & 2 & 3

Clap each of the following:

Re-write each of the above patterns in the space to the right using ♩. where possible.

How many times does ♩. ♪ ♩ occur in "Die Musici"?

1 & 2   &   3 &

Die Musici

German Round

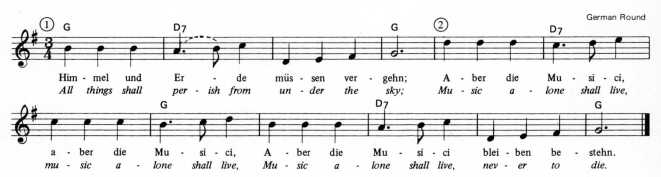

Him - mel und Er - de müs - sen ver - gehn; A - ber die Mu - si - ci,
All things shall per - ish from un - der the sky; Mu - sic a - lone shall live,

a - ber die Mu - si - ci, A - ber die Mu - si - ci blei - ben be - stehn.
mu - sic a - lone shall live, Mu - sic a - lone shall live, nev - er to die.

Clap the melodic rhythm as you tap the beat with your feet. What is the keynote? How is F played? Is there an anacrusis? A new pitch is needed to play this on the recorder, high E.

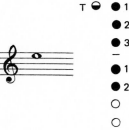

The tone is fingered like low E except the thumb hole on the back is only half coverd for the high E. You may need to adjust your thumb opening slightly for the high E to "speak" easily.

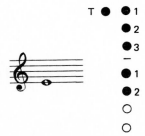

Practice playing between low E and high E.

Blow faster for the high E.

Improvise a short recorder piece using an uneven pattern with these two tones. Include other tones and rhythms if you wish.

Now practice playing D, high E, C as the pitches that occur in the second and third measures of the second line.

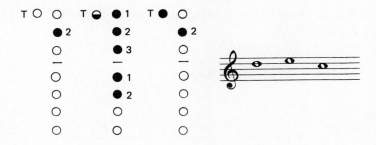

Play "Die Musici" on the recorder, taking care to execute the uneven pattern in measure two of each line correctly as:

♩. ♪ ♩
1 & 2 & 3 &

Sing "Die Musici."

Add the following descant on recorder. Which bars have uneven patterns? Where are the last four measures?

"Die Musici" is harmonized with only two chords. The $\frac{3}{4}$ meter may be emphasized on the guitar by picking on beat one and strumming on 2-3.

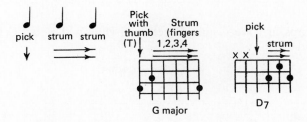

Practice this pattern until it is natural. Accompany your singing with this pattern.

The $\frac{3}{4}$ meter may be emphasized on the piano by playing with both hands.

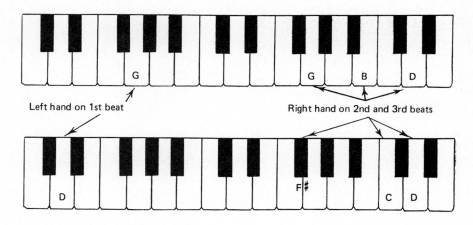

This is called the *root–chord* system of playing. Accompany your singing on the piano with this pattern. (Root–chord–chord)

How would you emphasize $\frac{2}{4}$ meter using the G and D_7 chords? $\frac{4}{4}$ meter? Practice both with guitar and piano.

Play "America" on the recorder.

America

How many different even patterns are there? Practice clapping each as you tap the beat. How many different uneven patterns are there? Practice these the same way.

What is the keynote of "America"? Is there an anacrusis? Play this descant to "America."

How many sharps in "We Gather Together"? How will F and C be played?

We Gather Together

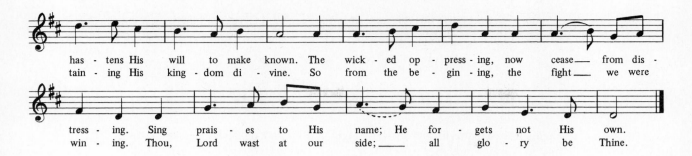

has - tens His will to make known. The wick - ed op - press - ing, now cease —— from dis -
tain - ing His king - dom di - vine. So from the be - gin - ing, the fight —— we were

tress - ing. Sing prais - es to His name; He for - gets not His own.
win - ing. Thou, Lord wast at our side; —— all glo - ry be Thine.

F♯ and C♯ in the key signature identify the key of D major. D is thus the key-note. What is the final tone? This is called the *tonic* tone, another name for the key-note. What is the tone of the anacrusis?

It is quite common to find a note five pitch names higher than the keynote as the anacrusis. (D–E–F♯–G–A). This is called the *dominant* tone. The dominant tone is second in importance to the tonic or keynote. It is the *interval* of a *fifth* higher than the tonic.

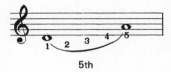

5th

When only one chord is used to harmonize a song, it is usually the one with the *tonic* as root. If a second chord is used, it is usually the one with the *dominant* as root.

Sing and play "We Gather Together," taking care to notice and play correctly each even and uneven pattern.

What is the keynote (tonic) of "America, the Beautiful"?

America, The Beautiful

Words by Katherine Lee Bates
Music by Samuel A. Ward

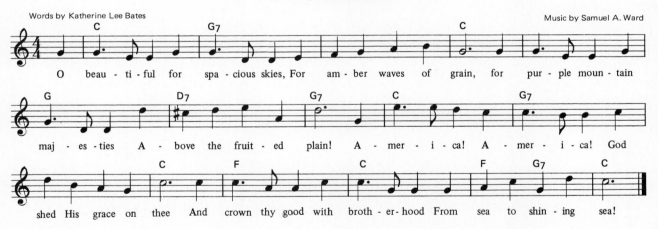

O beau - ti - ful for spa - cious skies, For am - ber waves of grain, for pur - ple moun - tain

maj - es - ties A - bove the fruit - ed plain! A - mer - i - ca! A - mer - i - ca! God

shed His grace on thee And crown thy good with broth - er - hood From sea to shin - ing sea!

The note G is five tones above C and is the dominant tone. (C–D–E–F–G) It is the interval of a fifth higher.

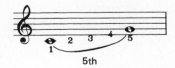

5th

What pitch is the anacrusis?

Practice clapping the uneven pattern in the second measure of each line against the even beat.

Pattern one   Clap   1   2   &   3   4

Pattern two   Tap

Patschen the first pattern on your left thigh, the second on your right thigh. Conduct a "four" pattern.

with your right hand as you snap the ♩. ♪ ♩ ♩ with your left fingers.

Improvise on your left thigh as you conduct a "four" pattern with your right hand.

Play "America, the Beautiful" on the recorder. What is the beginning count? (Note the accidental C♯ in measure three of line two. This note applies *only* for that measure. All other Cs are played natural ♮.)

Sing "America the Beautiful," tapping an even ♩ ♩ ♩ ♩ as you sing.

Is there an anacrusis in the theme from *Finlandia*? On what count does it begin? How many beats in the final measure?

Practice counting these uneven patterns.

In addition, there are some patterns which are neither even nor uneven. Practice these.

Play the theme from *Finlandia* on the recorder, remembering to blow lightly on notes in which all or most of the holes are covered. To begin, count

1   2   3   4 | 1   2   3   4 *etc.*

Theme
Finlandia

Jean Sibelius (1865–1957)

Write eight measures of rhythm in each of the following: $\frac{2}{4}$ $\frac{3}{4}$ $\frac{4}{4}$

Play a duet with someone else using sandblocks and jingle clogs.

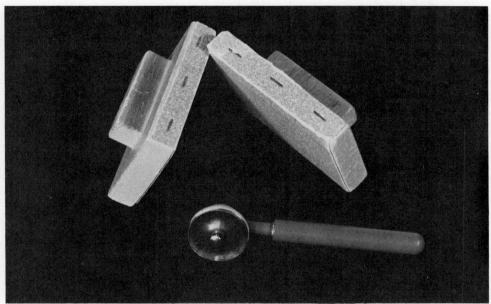

Photo by Donald Smith,
Slide City, Tucson, Arizona.

Sandblocks   **Jingle clogs**

All of the uneven patterns so far have been distributed over at least two beats in a long-short duration.

It is also possible to divide an uneven pattern over *one* beat. First, look how beats are divided evenly.

If ♩ = 1 count, then

73

An uneven division would result if three of the sixteenth notes were tied together.

1 e & a

This is most commonly written as  since

Thus,  or ═ , which is counted

1 a

Clap the following:

Compare it to

Re-write each of the following in the space provided at the right, using where possible. Clap each.

Study the following themes from the third movement of the

Third Symphony by Brahms (1833–1897)
(Bowmar Orchestral Library No. 71)

Which has the uneven pattern? Listen for the melodies. How are unity and variety achieved?

"SYMPHONY NO. 3" from The Bowmar Orchestral Library "Symphonic Movements No. 1" (No. 086) by Lucille Wood
Copyright ©1976 by Bowmar Noble, a division of Belwin–Mills Publishing Corp. Used With Permission. All Rights Reserved.

How many times does this pattern occur in "Christmas is Coming"?

1   2 a 3   4

74

How many times does this pattern occur?

1 2 & 3 4

Clap the melodic rhythm as you tap the beat with your foot.
 Play the melodic rhythm on jingle clogs and the beat on castanets.

Regular castanets   *Handle castanets*

Christmas is Coming

Lucille Wood

1. Christ - mas   is   com - ing,   Christ - mas   is   com - ing!   See   the   can - dles   glow.
2. Christ - mas   is   com - ing,   Christ - mas   is   com - ing!   Hear   the   sleigh - bells   ring!

Christ - mas   is   com - ing,   Christ - mas   is   com - ing!   Lights   a - cross   the   snow.
Christ - mas   is   com - ing,   Christ - mas   is   com - ing!   Hear   the   chil - dren   sing.

Play "Christmas is Coming" on the recorder. Notice how measures one and two
(also five and six) are similar. The rhythm is identical but the pitch movement is similar. Measure one begins on D, jumps the interval of a fourth to G, and then a third to
B.

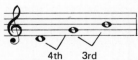

4th   3rd

Measure two begins on E, jumps a fourth to A and a third to C, the same intervals as
measure one. The only difference is the starting pitch of each measure.

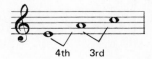

4th   3rd

75

When a melodic fragment, such as a measure, moves in the same direction and at the same intervals as another fragment, but begins on a different pitch, it is called a *sequence*. Sequences provide unity in music by repeating a rhythmic pattern and intervals at a different pitch level. A repeated rhythmic pattern such as ♩ ♫♩ ♩ is called a *motive*. (Return to "America, the Beautiful" and find a sequence.)

Sing "Christmas is Coming", accompanying yourself on the guitar or piano on this pattern. ♩   ♩ *etc.*

Emphasize ⁴⁄₄ on the guitar by using pick–strum–strum–strum. (♩ ♩ ♩ ♩)
On C major chord, this would be:

Pick on string 5 and strum downward on strings 4,3,2,1.

Emphasize ⁴⁄₄ on the piano by playing root–chord–chord–chord.
For C major chord, this pattern would be:

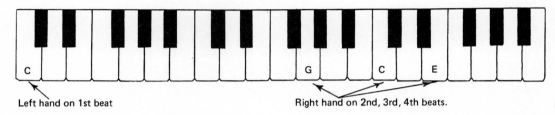

Left hand on 1st beat   Right hand on 2nd, 3rd, 4th beats.

Write several uneven patterns in ²⁄₄ ³⁄₄ ⁴⁄₄, using ♩. ♪ & ♩. ♪   Practice.

Improvise a short recorder melody using a sequence and uneven patterns.

"My White Mouse" uses both uneven patterns found in "Christmas is Coming."

Practice these rhythms:

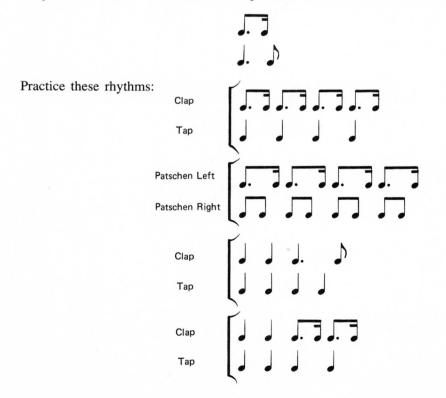

Now practice the melodic rhythm of "My White Mouse."

My White Mouse

English Words by Louise Kessler

German Folk Song

1. I have a cun - ning lit - tle mouse, his name is Jim, His
Refrain Now pat - ter pat - ter pat - ter on your tip - tip - toes, Your

name is Jim, his name is Jim. I have a cun - ning lit - tle mouse, his
tip - tip - toes, your tip - tip toes. Now pat - ter pat - ter pat - ter on your

name is Jim, And ev 'ry day I like to play with him.
tip - tip - toes, Little mouse, go danc - ing on your tip - tip - toes.

2. One night while I was sleeping, mousie ran away,
I looked for him, I looked for him.
One night while I was sleeping, mousie ran away.
I looked inside a shoe and there was Jim!

From MUSIC NOW AND LONG AGO. Copyright 1956, 1962 Silver Burdett Company. Reprinted by permission.

The anacrusis begins on the "and" of beat 4. (How many beats in the final measure?)

"I have"

1 2 3 4 & *etc.*

What is the keynote? What pitch is the anacrusis? What is the relationship between the two?

Play "My White Mouse" on recorder and sing.

This song may be accompanied on guitar using the pick–strum–strum–strum technique.

On piano, the root–chord–chord–chord pattern is:

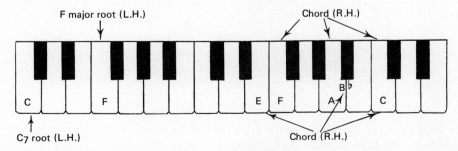

Study the even and uneven patterns in "Alouette" before performing it on the recorder. Sing and accompany on the piano, Autoharp, or guitar. Note the ‖: :‖ in the final line is repeated in each subsequent verse in order to add all the words. Also notice the D.C. al Fine.

Alouette

French Canadian Folk Song

A - lou - et - te,   gen - til' A - lou - et - te,   A - lou - et - te,   Je te plu - me - rai.

1. Je   te   plu - me - rai   la   tête,   Je   te   plu - me - rai   la   tête,
2. Je   te   plu - me - rai   le   bec,   Je   te   plu - me - rai   le   bec,

1. Et   la   tête,   et   la   tête,   A - lou - ette,   A - lou - ette,   O!
2. Et   le   bec,   et   le   bec,
3. Et   le   nez,   et   le   nez,

4. Le dos.   5. Les pattes.   6. Le cou.

"Gentil' Alouette" means "pretty meadow lark." "Je te plumerai" means "I shall pick off your feathers." 1. La tête: head. 2. Le bec: beak. 3. Le nez: nose. 4. Le dos: back. 5. Les pattes: feet. 6. Le cou: neck.

Uneven patterns in $\frac{6}{8}$ are much more common than even patterns. The most common even patterns are:

Uneven patterns result if the first two eighths of either grouping are tied together.

This is more commonly written as:

Find this pattern in "Summer is A-Coming In." Practice the melodic rhythm and perform on recorder. Sing on "loo" and perform as a round in three parts.

Summer is A-Coming In

English Melody (14th Century)

Not too fast

Find the same uneven pattern ♩♪♩♪ in Theme from the Pastorale Symphony. Practice the melodic rhythm, taking care to observe the tie in this pattern.

($\flat$ $\downarrow$ $\rlap{\raise1pt\hbox{$-$}}{\varepsilon}$· is neither even nor uneven since it is short-long.) (How is B played?)

Theme from Symphony No. 6 *(Pastorale)*

Allegretto   Ludwig van Beethoven (1770-1827)

Study the rhythms in "The Railroad Train." Play on the recorder. Sing and accompany on the guitar, Autoharp, and piano. The accompanying rhythm is ♩. ♩. duple.
1 2

The Railroad Train

Charles Harvey

1. Click-et-y clack, a-lunk, a-lunk! A train is com-ing, a-chunck, a-chunck; A
2. O-ver the bridge, a-cross the lake, A mile a min-ute it has to make; A

click-et-y clack a mile a-way; It has-'nt a sec-ond o'
ter-ri-ble snake, with flam-ing eyes, That wig-gles and wrig-gles a-

time to stay; It sings a nois-y clack-et-y song, A rick-et-y, rock-et-y,
long the ties, The cin-ders fall in fi-er-y rain, A tun-nel is wait-ing to

rack-et-y song, You're on the track, get out of the way, go 'long!____
swal-low the train, Good-bye, good-bye! To-mor-row he'll come a-gain!____

"Here We Come A-Wassailing" changes from $\frac{6}{8}$ to $\frac{2}{2}$. Basically it is duple throughout with the ♩. of the first two lines equalling the ♩ of the refrain. Find the even and uneven patterns in both sections. Play, sing, and accompany.

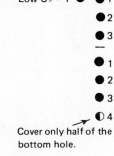

Low C♯ = T
Cover only half of the bottom hole.

Here We Come A-Wassailing

English Carol

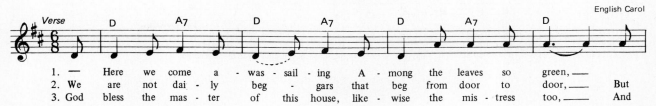

1. — Here we come a-was-sail-ing A-mong the leaves so green, ____
2. We are not dai-ly beg-gars that beg from door to door, ____ But
3. God bless the mas-ter of this house, like-wise the mis-tress too, ____ And

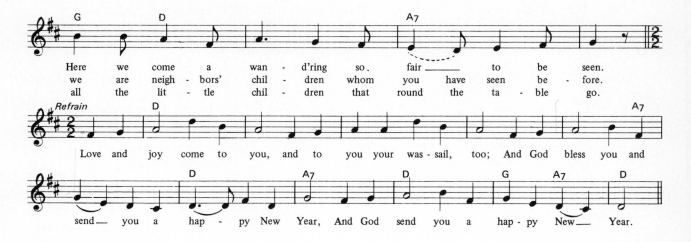

Here we come a wan - d'ring so, fair to be seen.
we are neigh - bors' chil - dren whom you have seen be - fore.
all the lit - tle chil - dren that round the ta - ble go.

Refrain

Love and joy come to you, and to you your was - sail, too; And God bless you and

send you a hap - py New Year, And God send you a hap - py New Year.

"Rig-a-Jig-Jig" changes from $\frac{2}{4}$ to $\frac{6}{8}$. Basically it remains duple throughout, but with the ♩ of the first two lines equalling the ♩. of the last two. Find the even and uneven patterns in both sections. Notice the use of G# in the refrain. This is fingered on the recorder as:

Play, sing, and accompany. Improvise a four measure introduction and coda for rhythm instruments using $\frac{6}{8}$ patterns.

Rig-A-Jig-Jig

English Folk Song

Verse

1. & 2. As I was walk - ing down the street, down the street, down the street, 1. A
2. A
pret - ty girl I chanced to meet, Hi - ho, hi - ho, hi - ho!
pret - ty boy

Refrain

1. & 2. Rig - a - jig - jig, and a - way we go, a - way we go, a way we go;

Rig - a - jig - jig, and a - way we go, Hi - ho, hi - ho, hi - ho.

Practice each of these lines. Play on classroom percussion. Play on select recorder tones or guitar/Autoharp/piano chords where appropriate.

Self-checking Chapter Review

Match Column II to Column I

1. _____
2. _____
3. _____
4. _____

(5 to 7 are fingerings, 8 to 10 are intervals)

5. _____
6. _____
7. _____ SEE ABOVE
8. _____
9. _____
10. _____
11. _____ motive

12. _____ tonic
13. _____ dominant
14. _____
15. _____ sequence
16. _____ contour
17. _____
18. _____
19. _____
20. _____ root

A. B. C.

D. keynote
E. foundation of chord
F. melodic direction
G. ♩ ♪ ♩ ♪
H. ♩ ♫ ♩ ♩. ♪
I. ♫
J. repeated rhythmic pattern
K. ♩. ♪ ♩ ♩
L. interval of a fourth
M. ♩. ♪ ♩
N. repetition of a melodic fragment
   at a higher or lower pitch
O. five notes higher than the tonic
P. ♩. ♩.
Q. ♩. ♪ ♩. ♪
R. interval of a fifth
S. ♩ ♪ ♩.
T. interval of a third

Melody	*enharmonic ~ chromatic scale*
Rhythm	*syncopation*
Harmony	*E♭ major ~ B♭ major ~ relative keys ~ parallel keys*
Form	*calypso ~ interlude ~ couplet*

Syncopation and syncopated patterns are a third type of movement over a basic beat. Unlike even or uneven division of rhythms, in syncopation a normal accent is shifted from where it is expected,

Accent shifted by note values from first to second beat.

or removed from its normal placement.

Accent removed from first beat.

Syncopation provides much interest and excitement in music because of its interplay with even and uneven rhythms.

    Clap the following. Which patterns are even? Uneven? Syncopated?

Syncopation, in contrast to the long-short division of uneven patterns, often results in a *short-long* division over a measure, beat, or fraction of a beat.

Listen to

Golliwog's Cakewalk by Debussy (1862–1918)
(Bowmar Orchestral Library No. 63)

The syncopation occurs in the main theme.

What tempos are used? How are unity and variety achieved?

Study the differences between these patterns. Clap each several times.

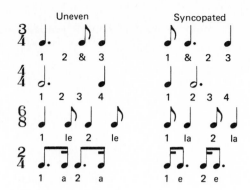

Ties are also used to create syncopation.

Write several even patterns. Change some to syncopated by adding ties.

Improvise syncopated patterns over a steady beat.
    Play "Vesper Hymn" in the first version. All patterns are even.

Version One

Vesper Hymn

Thomas Moore

Attributed to D. Bortniansky

Hark, the ves - per hymn is steal - ing   O'er the wa ters soft and clear.
Near - er yet and near - er peal - ing,   Soft it breaks up - on the ear.

Ju - bi - la - te!   Ju - bi - la - te!   Ju - bi - la - te!   A - men.

Clap the melodic rhythm of the second version of "Vesper Hymn," taking care to note which patterns are even, uneven, or syncopated.

Version Two

Patschen the melodic rhythm of version one on your left thigh as you patschen version two on your right thigh. Conduct $\frac{4}{4}$ as you sing version two. Play version two, tapping a steady $\frac{4}{4}$. In duet, play line one of version one against line two of version two. (Then line two of version one against line one of version two.)

Rewrite a song used in an earlier chapter so it incorporates at least *two* syncopated patterns. (You may improvise a syncopated version if you prefer.)

Where is the syncopation in "Mein Hut"? Count the following: Why is this syncopated?

1   2   3   1   2   3

Mein Hut

German

My hat it has three cor - ners; _____ Three cor - ners has my hat; _____ And
Mein Hut der hat drei Eck - en, _____ Drei Eck - en hat mein Hut; _____ Und

had it not three cor - ners; _____ it would not be my hat. _____
hat er nicht drei Eck - en; _____ Denn das ist nicht mein Hut. _____

Add the following descant on song bells, recorder, or piano.

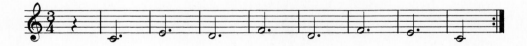

The finger and hand position for piano are:

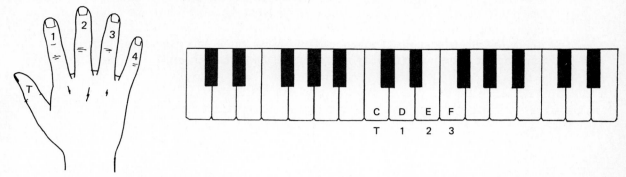

The C, G₇ (and F, which is not used here) patterns on the piano are played:

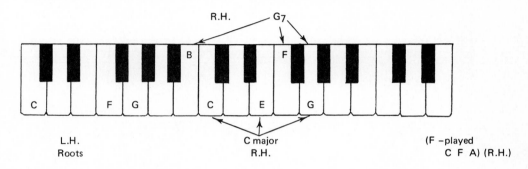

Accompany "Mein Hut" on the piano with singing and recorders.

Practice the piano in $\frac{3}{4}$ using root-chord-chord

and in $\frac{2}{4}$ using root-chord

and in $\frac{4}{4}$ using root-chord-chord-chord or
root-chord-root-chord

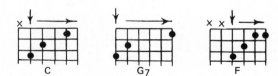

This can also be practiced on the guitar.

"My Lord What a Morning" includes three syncopated patterns:

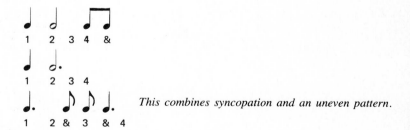

This combines syncopation and an uneven pattern.

Practice each against a steady movement of ♩ ♩ ♩ ♩

Sound the starting pitch on recorder or piano and sing "My Lord, What a Morning."

My Lord, What a Morning

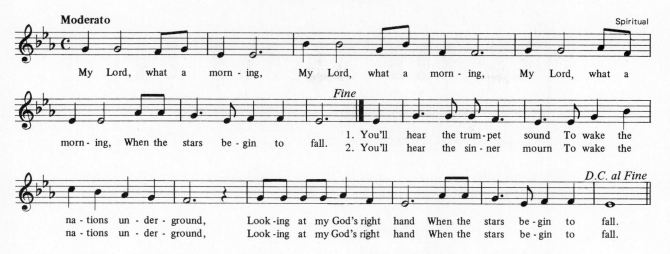

Three flats is the key signature in E♭ major, in which all Bs, Es, and As are played flat ♭.

Recorder fingerings for the new notes are:

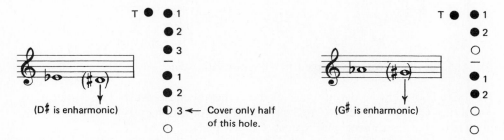

(D♯ is enharmonic)   ← Cover only half of this hole.

(G♯ is enharmonic)

Enharmonic notes are those that are spelled differently but sound and are played the same. (What other names may be given to sharp or flat notes you have learned earlier?)

Play "My Lord, What a Morning" on recorders.

It is now possible to play all notes within an octave on the recorder. The twelve half steps within an octave form the *chromatic* scale.

Play the following chromatic scale downward.

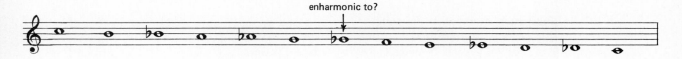

Reverse the chromatic scale and play upward.

Enharmonic notes in the chromatic scale are usually notated as flats (♭) in descending motion and sharps (♯) in ascending.

On the piano, the chromatic scale is:

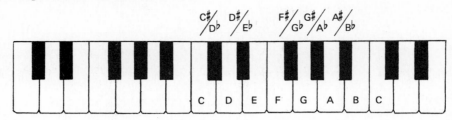

On the guitar, the same chromatic scale may be played:

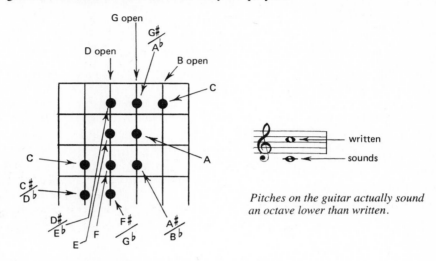

Pitches on the guitar actually sound an octave lower than written.

An Autoharp has strings arranged in the chromatic scale.

Playing a chord blocks out all tones of the chromatic scale except those used in the chord (i.e. C major chord = C E G strings only). An Autoharp is tuned by matching pitches on the instrument with a freshly tuned piano.

First tune all Cs (including octaves), then Gs, Fs, Ds, As, Bs, Es, and finally all ♭s and ♯s and their octaves.

Tune an Autoharp as a class project.

The syncopated patterns in "Nobody Knows the Trouble I've Seen" are:

Find each example in the song.

Nobody Knows the Trouble I've Seen

88

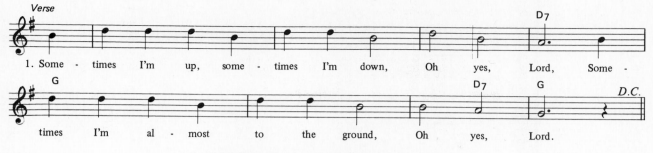

Verse

1. Some - times I'm up, some - times I'm down, Oh yes, Lord, Some -
times I'm al - most to the ground, Oh yes, Lord.

2. Although you see me going along slow, Oh, yes, Lord,
   I have great trials here below, Oh, yes, Lord.

3. One day when I was walking along, Oh, yes, Lord,
   Heaven opened wide, and love came down, Oh, yes, Lord.

4. Why does old Satan hate me so? Oh, yes, Lord,
   He had me once, then let me go, Oh, yes, Lord.

5. I never will forget the day, Oh, yes, Lord,
   When Jesus washed my sins away, Oh, yes, Lord.

From *Guitar in the Classroom*, 1971, Timmerman and Griffith (Dubuque: William C. Brown)

Sing and play on the recorder. Accompany on the guitar, Autoharp, and piano.

Notice the refrain occurs before the verse.

Play each of the following songs on the recorder and sing. Which patterns are syncopated?

Riding in the Buggy

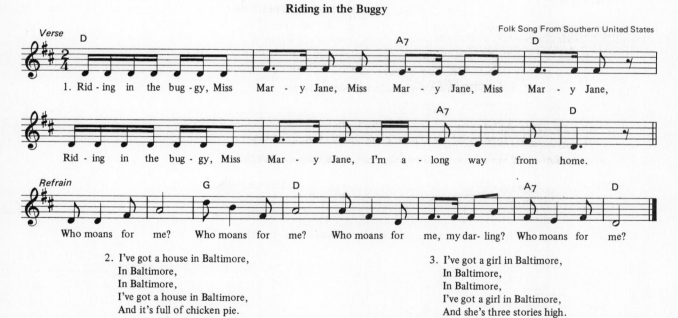

Folk Song From Southern United States

Verse

1. Rid - ing in the bug - gy, Miss Mar - y Jane, Miss Mar - y Jane, Miss Mar - y Jane,
Rid - ing in the bug - gy, Miss Mar - y Jane, I'm a - long way from home.

Refrain

Who moans for me? Who moans for me? Who moans for me, my dar - ling? Who moans for me?

2. I've got a house in Baltimore,
   In Baltimore,
   In Baltimore,
   I've got a house in Baltimore,
   And it's full of chicken pie.

3. I've got a girl in Baltimore,
   In Baltimore,
   In Baltimore,
   I've got a girl in Baltimore,
   And she's three stories high.

89

Time for Work

Lively

Israeli Folk Song

Morn - ing, morn - ing, is the time for work;__ Morn - ing, morn - ing, is the time for work;

Noon - time, noon - time, is the time for eat - ing; Eve - ing, time for rest; Night - time for sleep - ing.

Persian Rhythm

English Words by Sally Monsour

Transcribed by Manoochehr Sadeghi

Danc - ing rhy - thm, and beat; stamp rhy - thm, and beat. Danc - ing rhy - thm,

and beat; stamp rhy - thm, and beat. Clap - ping, clap - ping, clap - ping__ rhy - thm;

clap to - geth - er, each one__ tries. Join us as we sing in__ rhy - thm;

smil - ing__ fac - es, flash - ing__ eyes. Danc - ing rhy - thm, and beat; stamp rhy - thm,

and beat, Danc - ing rhy - thm, and beat; stamp rhy - thm, and beat.

Used by permission of Sally Monsour.

Where are pitches the same? Conjunct? Disjunct?

John the Rabbit

American Folk Song Game
Collected by John W. Work

Old John the rab - bit, Oh, yes! Old John the rab - bit, Oh, yes! Got a might - y bad hab - bit,

Oh, yes! Of go - ing to my gar - den, Oh, yes! And eat - ing up my peas,

Oh, yes! And cut - ting down my cab - bage, Oh, yes! He ate to - ma - toes, Oh, yes! And

sweet po - ta - toes, Oh, yes! And if I live, Oh, yes! To see next fall,

Oh, yes! I won't plant, Oh, yes! A gar - den at all!

Accompany on guitar and piano. Root-chord on piano is:

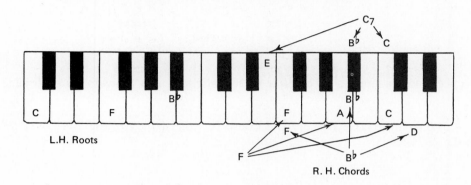

Caught a Rabbit

Kentucky Folk Song
Collected by Jean Thomas, The "Traipsin' Woman"

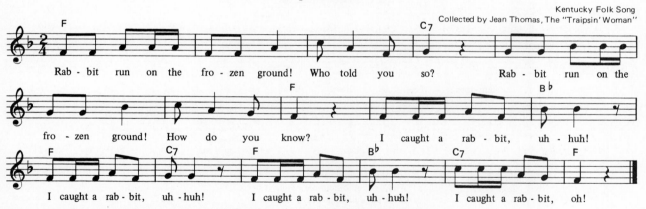

Rab - bit run on the fro - zen ground! Who told you so? Rab - bit run on the

fro - zen ground! How do you know? I caught a rab - bit, uh - huh!

I caught a rab - bit, uh - huh! I caught a rab - bit, uh - huh! I caught a rab - bit, oh!

Listen to

Infernal Dance of Koschai by Stravinsky (1882–1971)
(Bowmar Orchestral Library No. 69)

Why is this theme syncopated?

Allegro

What instruments do you hear? How does this aid unity and variety?

Syncopation frequently occurs *within* one beat rather than being spread over two or more beats. In one beat, the most important note usually occurs *exactly* on the beat. If this is changed, syncopation results.

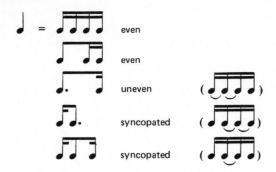

Practice these patterns and by patsching, with your left hand.

Clap the melodic rhythm of "Old House" as you tap the pulse. Sing and play on the recorder.

Old House

American Folk Game Song
Collected by John W. Work

1. Old house. Tear it down! Who's going to help me? Tear it down!
Bring me a ham-mer. Tear it down! Bring me a saw.___ Tear it down!
Next thing you bring me, Tear it down! Is a wreck-ing ma-chine. Tear it down!

2. New house. Build it up!
Who's going to help me? Build it up!
Bring me a hammer. Build it up!
Bring me a saw. Build it up!
Next thing you bring me, Build it up!
Is a carpenter man. Build it up!

Calypso music from the West Indies is often full of syncopation. Find examples in "Tinga Layo."

Tinga Layo

Calypso Song From the West Indies

Tin - ga Lay - o! Come, lit - tle don - key, come; Tin - ga Lay - o! Come, lit - tle don - key, come.

1. My don-key walk, my don-key talk, my don-key eat with a knife and fork.
2. My don-key eat, my don-key sleep, my don-key kick with his two hind feet. Tin - ga Lay - o!

Come, lit - tle don-key, come; Tin - ga Lay - o! Come, lit - tle don-key, come.

Play on the recorder and sing. Accompany on harmony instruments.

Calypso music is often accompanied by Latin American rhythm instruments. Add these patterns as you sing and play.

Cymbals and Finger cymbals   *Photo by Donald Smith,*
Slide City, Tucson, Arizona.

Write your own calypso patterns and add to the song. Improvise an eight measure introduction, an eight measure *interlude*, a musical filler (between verses one and two), and an eight measure coda.

Study each of the following songs for keynote and rhythm patterns. Play each on the recorder, sing and accompany with harmony and rhythm instruments.

Hey Lidee

3. What do we do when summer ends?
   Hey Lidee, Lidee-lo.
   We go to school and make new friends,
   Hey Lidee, Lidee-lo. *(Refrain)*

4. What can we do when music comes,
   Hey Lidee, Lidee-lo.
   We'll play the drums and sing our songs,
   Hey Lidee, Lidee-lo. *(Refrain)*

Words and music by James Leisy ©Copyright MCMLXVI, MCMLXXV, Shawnee Press, Inc., Delaware Water Gap, PA 18327. International Copyright Secured. All Rights Reserved. Used with permission.

Improvise new verses as suggested by verses two and three. You need a couplet, that is, two rhyming lines.

Line 1 _____
Hey Lidee, Lideelo. } couplet
Line 2 _____
Hey Lidee, Lideelo.

Round the Bay of Mexico

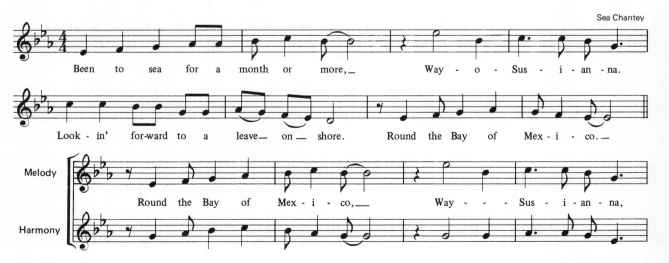

Mex - i - co's the place— I be - long in, Round the Bay of Mex - i - co.—

Add calypso patterns to both of the above songs.

''Rock Island Line'' has two flats (B♭ and E♭) in the key signature. This means the keynote is B♭ and the song's tonality is B♭ major. Play the melody (bottom line) on the recorder. Sing. Add the top line ostinato on a melody instrument.

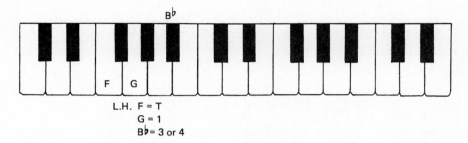

L.H. F = T
      G = 1
      B♭= 3 or 4

On xylophone or metallophone, using mallets.
On the piano.

Metallophone   *Xylophone*   *Photo by Donald Smith,*
                                                     Slide City, Tucson, Arizona.

Pattern of playing mallets.
    Practice on thigh first.

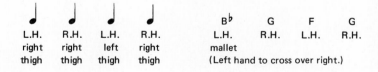

L.H.	R.H.	L.H.	R.H.	B♭	G	F	G
right	right	left	right	L.H.	R.H.	L.H.	R.H.
thigh	thigh	thigh	thigh	mallet			
				(Left hand to cross over right.)			

Write or improvise other ostinatos in $\frac{4}{4}$ with the above pitches. Add an introduction and coda.

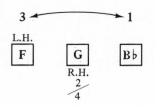

Rock Island Line

From *Growing with Music,* Wilson, et al., Book 5 (Englewood Cliffs, NJ: Prentice–Hall, Inc., 1966)

Keyed percussion instruments like the xylophone and metallophone are basic to a system of music training developed by the German composer Carl Orff (1895–1982). Ostinatos are created as accompaniment to tunes like "Rock Island Line." Orff principles have been incorporated into many elementary and secondary schools in the United States.

Practice each of these lines. Play on classroom percussion. Play on select recorder tones or guitar/Autoharp/piano chords where appropriate.

Several key signatures have been introduced. What keynote (tonic) is represented by each of the following:

All of the above key signatures are major keys. In reality, each key signature may represent a *major* tonality or a different *minor* tonality, which is called the *relative minor*.

The key signature of no sharps and no flats may be either C major *or* a minor. The following song, "Joshua Fought the Battle of Jericho," is in a minor. Find and practice all syncopated patterns.

Joshua Fought the Battle of Jericho

From *Guitar in the Classroom,* 1971, Timmerman and Griffith (Dubuque: William C. Brown)

Sing and accompany on the guitar using a minor and E_7. Use a pick-strum pattern in $\frac{4}{4}$.

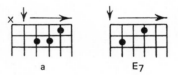

Piano chords are:

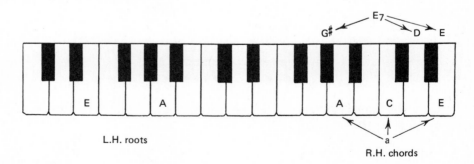

The relative minor key for each of the above major tonalities is:

Relative majors and minors have the same key signature. An analysis of the song (i.e. beginning and ending pitches and predominant chords) ultimately tells whether the song is major or minor. *Parallel* major and minor keys, however, have the *same* key-note (C major and c minor, G major and g minor, etc.) but *different* key signatures.

Play and sing "The First Nowell," which is in D major. The new recorder note in the descant is high F♯:

The First Nowell

Traditional

1. The first Now - ell, the an - gels did say, Was to
2. They look - ed up and saw a star Shin - ing

cer - tain poor shep - herds in fields as they lay, In
in the East be - yond them a - far, And

fields where they lay keep - ing their sheep On a
to the earth it gave a great light, And

cold win - ter's night that was so deep.
so it con - tin - ued both day and night.

Refrain
Descant

Now - ell, Now - ell, Now - ell, now - ell,

Born is the King of Is - ra - el.

high F♯

Now compare this with the same song written in the parallel minor. The key signature has been changed, which affects Fs, Cs, and Bs. The new recorder note in the descant is now high F♮:

Now play all chromatic notes on the recorder from high F♯ to middle C. Only one new tone is needed.

Listen to

Funeral March of a Marionette by Gounod (1818–1893)
(Bowmar Orchestral Library No. 64)

Theme one is in minor.

Theme two is in the parallel major.

Theme one returns in the final section. How many sections are there? What effect does the return of theme one have?

Self-checking Chapter Review

Match Column II (on the next page) with Column I.

1. _____
2. _____
3. _____
4. _____
5. _____
6. _____
7. _____

8. _____ ⎤
9. _____ ⎟
10. _____ SEE ABOVE
11. _____ ⎦

What is the keynote of:

12. _____ ⎤
13. _____ ⎟
14. _____ ⎟
15. _____ SEE ABOVE
16. _____ ⎟
17. _____ ⎦

18. _____

19. _____

20. _____ enharmonic to E♭

A. B. C. D.

E. ♪ ♩ ♪ ♩

F. ♪ ♩. ♩

G. ♪ ♩ ♪ ♩ ♩

H. ♫ ♩ ♫

I. ♩ ♩.

J. ♪ ♩ ♪ ♫

K. ♫. ♫ ♩

L. E₇

M. C

N. G

O. D♯

P. a minor

Q. B♭

R. E♭

S. D

T. F

Complete the following crossword puzzle.

Across

1. Type of pattern this is: ♪ ♩ ♪ ♩ ♩
3. Relative minor of C major.
4. Play with the root.
5. Syllable to sing on.
6. Type of pattern this is: ♩. ♪ ♩ ♩
*10. Abbreviation for "very loud."
11. ♭
13. A note to follow "sol."
14. Keynote
15. Type of pattern this is: ♫ ♩ ♫ ♩ ♩
16. either _____
17. dis _____
18. Piece for one.

Down

2. Two rhyming lines.
4. Type of bell for calypso.
7. Relative minor of G major.
8. Calypso instrument.
*9. Abbreviation for "medium loud."
*10. Abbreviation for "loud."
11. Relative major of d minor.
12. Interval between middle C and 4th space E, a _____th.

*See pages 103-104.

Melody	phrase ~ cadence ~ period ~ bass clef ~ grand staff
Rhythm	triplet ~ duplet
Harmony	E major
Dynamics	dynamic markings ~ crescendo ~ decrescendo
Form	repetition ~ contrast ~ strophic ~ rondo ~ stanza ~ ballad

To be music, sound needs design. Design in music is referred to as *form*. The basic premise in form is that music must have some *repetition* to give it unity. However, all repetition or unity could lead to a dull design, so *contrast* provides continuing interest and variety. Contrast is accomplished by slightly altering an original idea or including new ones. The delicate balance between repetition and contrast, unity and variety, is the essence of form. It applies to the simple folk song as well as a long symphonic movement.

Play "The More We Get Together" on the recorder.

Words Anonymous

The More We Get Together

Old German Melody

This simple song has four *phrases*. A phrase is defined in music as a melodic unit which is coherent and relatively complete. In singing, a phrase is about a "breath" length, which each of these is. If phrase No. 1 is used as a reference, how does No. 2 compare? Is it identical? Similar? Different? How does No. 3 compare? No. 4?

Sing "The More We Get Together." The form, by phrases, is:

1st phrase, unity—call this phrase A

2nd phrase, similar to the first—call this phrase A_1

3rd phrase, different—call this phrase B

4th phrase, identical to No. 2 and similar to No. 1—call this phrase A_1

By phrases, then, the form is $AA_1 BA_1$.

Form may be reinforced by intensity. Notice the dynamic markings at the beginning of each phrase:

mf = medium loud (mezzo forte)

f = loud (forte)

ff = very loud (fortissimo)

"Soft" in music may be indicated in a similar manner:

mp = medium soft (mezzo piano)
p = soft (piano)
pp = very soft (pianissimo)

Arranged in a continuum, these six dynamic markings are:

soft ←——————————————————————————→ loud
pp   *p*   *mp*   *mf*   *f*   *ff*

The following form is a *rondo*. A rondo is a composition that has a recurring idea which begins and usually ends the work. In addition, it appears throughout the movement interspersed between other material. The form of this rondo by phrases is A B A C A.

Perform it, observing the dynamic markings of each section.

Rondos may also be organized as A B A, A B A B A, and A B A C A B A. Write a rondo in one of these designs, making each section at least eight measures in length. Indicate dynamic markings.

Dynamic changes in music are effected in several ways. In singing, playing the recorder or strumming the guitar, more energy is needed to sound louder. This may mean speeding up the air velocity as one sings or blows or strumming with more pressure on the guitar. Playing louder on the piano also means touching with more pressure. To a certain degree, the number of persons and instruments singing or playing also affects the relative loudness or softness of tone.

Repeat "The More We Get Together," carefully observing the dynamic marking of each phrase.

There are two phrases in "Three Dukes." What is the overall form?

Three Dukes

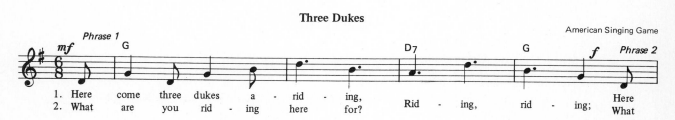

American Singing Game

1. Here come three dukes a - rid - ing, Rid - ing, rid - ing; Here
2. What are you rid - ing here for? What

come three dukes a - rid - ing,
are you rid - ing here for? Ran - som, pran - som, tan - tar - ry - O!

3. We're riding here to be married,
4. And which of us will you have, sirs?
5. You're all too slow and clumsy,
6. We're just as spry as you are,

7. You're all as stiff as pokers,
8. We can bend as well as you can,
9. The prettiest one is this one,

Sing and play "Three Dukes," observing the dynamic markings.

A phrase ends with a punctuation point called *a cadence*. A cadence is the breathing point where there is a slight feeling of repose in the music. A song with two phrases will have two cadences.

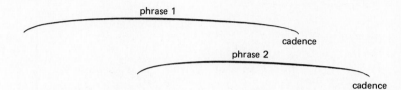

"Three Dukes" has a melody that is repeated over and over for additional verses of the song. This is called *strophic* form and is very typical of simple folk songs. Melody and harmony are repeated as the words change. Although this example has two phrases, strophic form may have any number of phrases.

Sing and play "Patsy."

Patsy

American Railroad Song

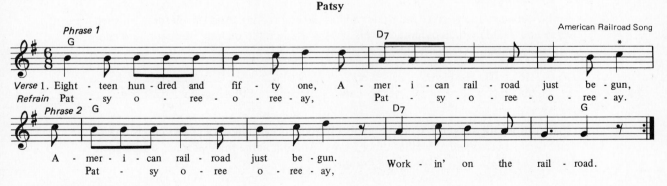

Verse 1. Eigh - teen hun - dred and fif - ty one, A - mer - i - can rail - road just be - gun,
Refrain Pat - sy o - ree - o - ree - ay, Pat - sy o - ree - o - ree - ay.

A - mer - i - can rail - road just be - gun. Work - in' on the rail - road.
Pat - sy o - ree o - ree - ay,

Eighteen hundred and fifty -
2. two, Lookin' around for things to do, . . . *(Refrain)*
3. three, The railroad comp'ny accepted me, . . . *(Refrain)*
4. four, I found my back was mighty sore, . . . *(Refrain)*
5. five, I found myself more dead than alive, . . . *(Refrain)*
6. six, I stepped on a pile of dynamite sticks, . . . *(Refrain)*
7. seven, I found myself on the way to Heav'n, . . . *(Refrain)*
8. eight, I was pickin' the lock at the pearly gate, . . . *(Refrain)*
9. nine, I was floatin' around on the clouds sublime, . . . *(Refrain)*

There are two phrases here, A and A₁, like "Three Dukes." Also, like "Three Dukes," when all verses are performed, the overall form is strophic.

Since there are two phrases, there are also two cadences. Play or sing phrase one only. Does it sound complete? Phrases that end like this do not sound complete. The cadence helps explain this. In the melody, the first phrase ends on C, which is *not* the keynote.* The harmony is D_7, which is the chord built on the dominant tone (Keynote = G, dominant = D). This is an *incomplete* cadence since it does not sound finished. The song would not sound "finished" if it ended here.

Phrase two, however, ends on both pitch G and the tonic (G) chord. This gives a feeling of finality to the entire song. This type of cadence is called *complete*.

In general, a *complete* cadence is one in which the melody ends on the keynote and the harmony returns to I (tonic chord).

By contrast, an *incomplete* cadence is one in which the melody ends on *other* than the keynote. The harmony may or may not be on I. V_7 is very typical for incomplete cadences.

Complete the following chart to identify complete cadences.

Key	Melody note	Harmony
C major	C	C chord (I)
F major		
G major		
D major		
B♭ major		
E♭ major		

If a cadence ends on another melody pitch and/or has a V_7 chord, it is probably an incomplete cadence.

Repeat "Patsy," using the following as an introduction on song bells,

Add it between each verse (interlude) and at the end (coda). Add this descant on each verse and decide which dynamic levels will be used on the melody, descant, and subsequent verses.

The form is still strophic. Composers use introductions, interludes, and codas to extend works in strophic as well as other forms. Another name for a strophic song which tells a story, such as "Patsy," is *ballad*.

Where are the cadences in "Little Bird On My Window"? What characterizes the incomplete cadence (i.e. melody note and chord)?

Little Bird on My Window

Edith Krohner

German Folk Melody

1. Lit - tle bird on my win - dow, Will you sing me a song?

When you fly o - ver mea - dows, will you take me a - long?

2. There are beautiful flowers
I can see from my door,
But if I could go flying,
I would see many more.

3. So come back to my window,
Let your song never end.
I will tell you a secret,
You're a very good friend.

Play and sing "Little Bird on My Window," observing the dynamic markings. *This is an example of an incomplete cadence that ends on the I chord. The melody pitch, however is C (not the keynote F), which gives a feeling of incompleteness.

Decide on a dynamic level. Then play and sing "The Muffin Man."

The Muffin Man

English Singing Game

1. O do you know the muf - fin man, The muf - fin man, the muf - fin man, O do you know the muf - fin man, That lives in Dru - ry Lane?
2. O yes, I know the muf - fin man, The muf - fin man, the muf - fin man, O yes, I know the muf - fin man, That lives in Dru - ry Lane.

Where are the cadences and what type are they?

Two phrases are often paired to create a *period* in music. A period consists of a "questioning" phrase ending on an incomplete cadence.

"O do you know the muffin man, the muffin man, the muffin man," [*incomplete cadence*]

This phrase is called an *antecedent* or question. In a period, the antecedent is followed by an answering phrase, the *consequent,* which gives a feeling of finality since it terminates on a complete cadence.

"O do you know the muffin man, That lives in Drury Lane?" [*complete cadence*]

Write or improvise a consequent to the following antecedent. Include dynamic markings. Add words. Ending words of phrases can rhyme.*

Do the same for this antecedent.

Write an antecedent for the given consequent.

107

Play and sing what you have written.
Play and sing "White Coral Bells."

White Coral Bells

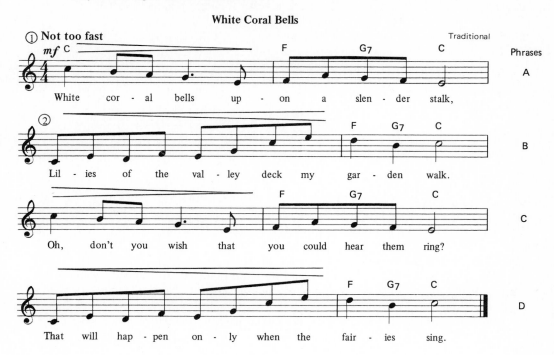

What is the form by phrases? Which cadences are incomplete? Complete? Two new dynamic markings are used:

or *crescendo,* which means to become louder gradually; and

or *decrescendo,* or *diminuendo,* which means to soften gradually.
"White Coral Bells" has a double period:

antecedent-consequent	AB
antecedent-consequent	CD

Perform it as a two–part round. Phrases and cadences now overlap, but the entire structure remains the same. Notice the harmony of each phrase is identical.

Measure 1	Measure 2
C	| F G$_7$ C

Rounds may be sung or played together because the harmony of each phrase is identical. The simplest rounds may be accompanied entirely by one chord, most frequently the I. More complex rounds, such as "White Coral Bells," change chords within the phrase.

Write a two phrase round, using the chords marked in each measure. End phrase one with an incomplete cadence, phrase two with a complete cadence. Begin and end on the keynote.

108

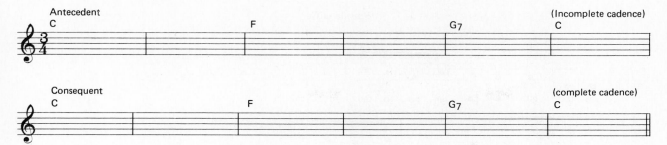

Practice each of the following songs, identifying phrases, cadences and periods (including antecedents and consequents.)

Jig Along Home

Words and Music by Woody Guthrie

TRO © Copyright 1951 and renewed 1979 Folkways Music Publishers, Inc., New York, NY. Used by permission.

One More River

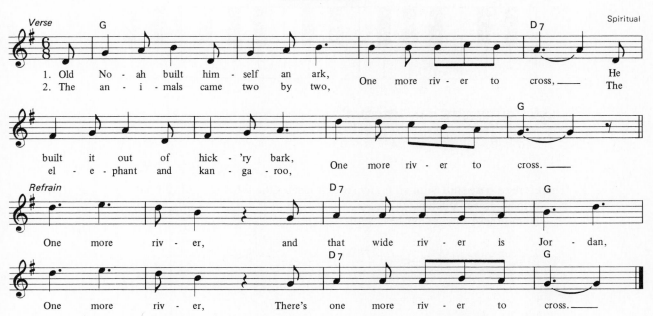

Spiritual

3. The animals came three by three,
   One more river to cross.
   The baboon and the chimpanzee,
   One more river to cross.

4. The animals came four by four,
   One more river to cross.
   The hippopotamus got stuck in the door,
   One more river to cross.

5. The animals came five by five,
   One more river to cross.
   The bees came swarming from the hive,
   One more river to cross.

From *Growing With Music,* Wilson, et al., Book 5 (Englewood Cliffs, NJ: Prentice–Hall, Inc. 1966)

Simple Gifts

'Tis the gift to be sim-ple, 'tis the gift to be free, 'Tis the gift to come down where you ought to be, And when we find our-selves in the place just right, 'Twill be in the val-ey of love and de-light. When true sim-plic-i-ty is gained, To bow and to bend we shan't be a-shamed, To turn, turn will be our de-light, Till by turn-ing, turn-ing we come out right.

Add harmony on guitar, Autoharp, and piano. Improvise rhythmic introductions, interludes and codas.

Although the treble staff is used to notate many pitches on the piano, pitches below middle C necessitate using too many ledger lines.

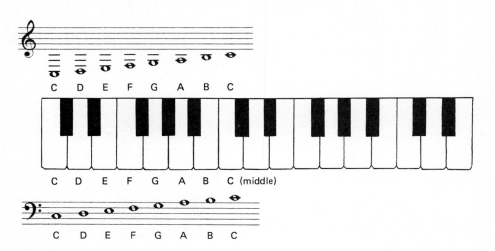

Therefore, a bass staff with an *F clef* (which locates the F below middle C) is used to notate these lower pitches.

Name these pitches on bass staff.

110

Lower-pitched band and orchestral instruments, such as the bassoon, trombone, tuba, etc, use this staff to avoid reading on ledger lines. On the piano, the right hand uses the treble staff, the left hand the bass. Together, the two staffs comprise the *grand staff*.

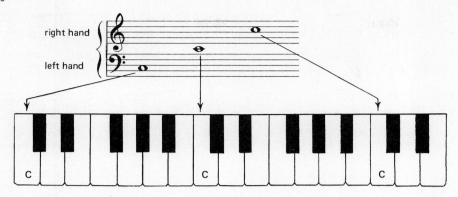

Root-chord patterns on the piano may be notated on the grand staff in this manner. Practice each in duple, triple and quadruple time.

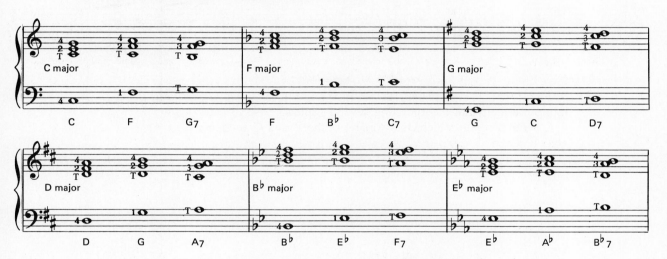

"The Linden Tree" is in the key of E major (4 sharps = E major, in which all Fs, Cs, Gs, and Ds are sharp).

 is a triplet, which means to play three notes in the time of two.

The triplet allows the composer to subdivide the beats into threes (in simple meter) instead of the customary two.

Play and sing "The Linden Tree."

The Linden Tree

Translated by H.G. Trebilcox

Music by Franz Schubert (1797–1828)

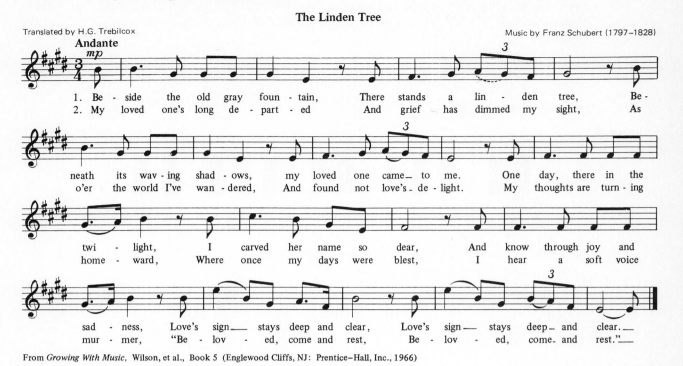

1. Be - side the old gray foun - tain, There stands a lin - den tree, Be -
2. My loved one's long de - part - ed And grief has dimmed my sight, As

neath its wav - ing shad - ows, my loved one came to me. One day, there in the
o'er the world I've wan - dered, And found not love's de - light. My thoughts are turn - ing

twi - light, I carved her name so dear, And know through joy and
home - ward, Where once my days were blest, I hear a soft voice

sad - ness, Love's sign stays deep and clear, Love's sign stays deep and clear.
mur - mer, "Be - lov - ed, come and rest, Be - lov - ed, come and rest."

From *Growing With Music,* Wilson, et al., Book 5 (Englewood Cliffs, NJ: Prentice–Hall, Inc., 1966)

Improvise a rhythm incorporating several triplets.
Write a rondo which uses triplets in the B and C sections.

A
B
A
C
A
B
A

Incorporate dynamic markings and perform on rhythm instruments, assigning a different timbre for each section.

Listen to

The Sea and Sinbad's Ship by Rimsky-Korsakoff (1844–1908)
(Bowmar Orchestral Library No. 77)

There are several themes. Which use triplets? What instruments play each theme?
Why is this an example of program music?

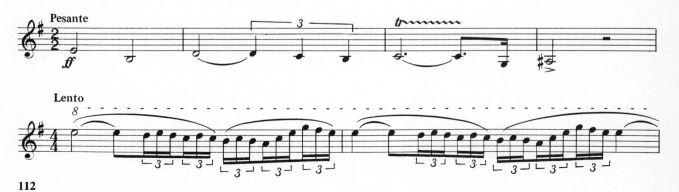

In compound meter, where the beat division is ordinarily three, a *duplet* may be used to divide the beat into two instead of three.

Practice each of these lines. Play on classroom percussion. Play on select recorder tones or guitar/Autoharp/piano chords where appropriate.

What is the form by phrase of "The Linden Tree"? Accompany it on the guitar and piano.

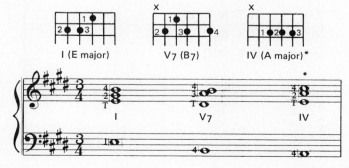

Self-checking Chapter Review

Identify each of the following.

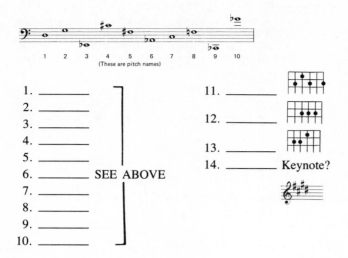

1. _____
2. _____
3. _____
4. _____
5. _____
6. _____ SEE ABOVE
7. _____
8. _____
9. _____
10. _____

11. _____
12. _____
13. _____
14. _____ Keynote?

Find a word in the ''word find'' that means the following. Answers may be horizontal, vertical, diagonal and forward and backward.

1. medium loud
2. medium soft
3. *ff*
4. *pp*
5. ABACABA
6. complete and incomplete
7. breath length
8. what an antecedent is
9. what a consequent is
10. ⟨
11. 𝄢 = F
12. 2 staffs together
13. ♩♪♪
14. antecedent + consequent =
15. musical ending
16. ♪♪

```
M E Z Z O F O R T E
E A K C J O E V V H
Z P B A I R T L G Z
Z E G D W T R S C F
O R R E C I E D E N
P I A N I S S I M O
I O N C X S A Q D I
A D D E L I R M U T
N C O D A M H Y P S
O D N O R O P A L E
T E L P I R T N E U
A N S W E R A O T Q
O D N E C S E R C P
```

Melody	pentatonic scale ~ hand signals
Form	echo song ~ theme and variations ~ antiphonal ~ partner song

A scale is a catalog of pitches from which a song is created. The chromatic scale is one such catalog, consisting entirely of half–steps, 12 to the octave.

The *pentatonic* scale is a five-toned scale. Although any five different pitches constitute a pentatonic scale, the most common one is:

The interval between the

first and second tone = whole step
second and third tone = whole step
third and fourth tone = whole plus half step
fourth and fifth tone = whole step
fifth and sixth tone = whole plus half step.

Play this pentatonic scale downward and then upward on the recorder.

Sing it on *loo*. The keynote is C, but the key is neither C major nor C minor. Rather, it is C pentatonic. Each note of this pentatonic scale may be represented by a syllable, *do-re-me-sol-la* (and *high do'*) respectively.

In a similar manner, each syllable may be represented by a hand signal (devised by John Curwen, an Englishman, in the Nineteenth century). The pentatonic scale and hand signals are integral to a system of music education developed by the Hungarian composer Zoltán Kodály (1882–1967). This system, like that of Carl Orff, has become very popular in the United States.

Using C as *do,* play the following exercise on the recorder and then sing, using syllables and hand signals.

115

Create several rhythms incorporating even, uneven and syncopated patterns. Add syllables from C pentatonic. Play on the recorder and then sing with syllables, using the hand signals.

Improvise melodies on the recorder using C pentatonic pitches.

Write a duet using C pentatonic pitches. Perform together. Pentatonic melodies are not dissonant when performed together because there are no half steps between adjacent tones.

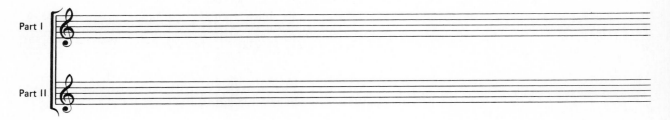

Play and sing "It's Raining."

It's Raining

Eunice Boardman and Beth Landis. *Exploring Music 1*, 1966, Holt, Rinehart and Winston, Inc. Reprinted by permission.

This is an incomplete C pentatonic scale, using only *la-sol-mi*.

Sing with syllables and hand signals.

Create new words about raining.

Ostinatos are easily added to pentatonic melodies, using the same five tones. Add this ostinato to "It's Raining" on recorder, piano, guitar, or xylophone, or sing it.

Use the ostinato as an introduction, interlude (between verses) and coda. Improvise several more ostinatos.

Play "Sail, Silver Moon Boat" on the recorder. This is also an incomplete C pentatonic, using *do'-la-sol*.

Sing with syllables and hand signals.

Sail, Silver Moon Boat

Chinese melody

1. See the sil - ver moon in the sky gen - tly float, Near the shin - ing stars, see the
2. Shine on sil - ver moon in the clouds so —— white, Shine on sil - ver moon with your

moon like a boat; Sail, sil - ver moon boat to the west, Sail, sil - ver moon boat while I rest.
smile so —— bright; Sail, sil - ver moon boat to the west, Sail, sil - ver moon boat while I rest.

Reprinted by permission of D.C. Heath and Company.

Create ostinatos using the other tones of the C pentatonic scale.

Add words. Play and sing these with the main song. Use the piano and guitar if possible.

Add these ostinato parts as accompaniment. Work out an introduction, interlude, and coda. Let someone direct in $\frac{4}{4}$.

Play "Hear the Echo" on recorder.

Hear the Echo

Words and Music by Richard Berg

Hear the ech - o!   Loud and clear!   Ech - o,   Ech - o,
Hear the ech - o!   Loud and clear!   Ech - o,   Ech - o,

Far and near!   Way up   on the   moun - tain   side,   side,   side.
Far and near!   Way up   on the   moun - tain - side,   side,   side.

Reprinted by permission of D.C. Heath and Company.

Sing with syllables and hand signals. Perform as a duet. This is an example of an *echo song* since line two imitates line one. The following is a variation on "Hear the Echo." What has been changed? Is it pentatonic?

Variations by J. O'Brien

Play and sing this variation as an echo song.
What has been changed in this variation? Play it. Is it pentatonic?

What has been changed in this variation? Play it. Is it pentatonic?

Write and then perform your own variation, changing one or more elements.

A *theme and variations* is a musical form in which a melody is first heard, followed by melodic, rhythmic, and harmonic changes, as well as changes in dynamics and timbre.

Listen to

Theme and Variations from the *Surprise Symphony* by Haydn (1732–1809)
(Bowmar Orchestral Library No. 62)

Two fragments from the theme are:

Four variations follow. What is the character of each variation?

The G pentatonic scale is:

d   r   m   s   l   d'

F♯ may or may not be placed in the key signature. This does not affect the scale. Although an F♯ is not used in G pentatonic, its placement in the key signature does signal a keynote of G. Play this scale on the recorder.

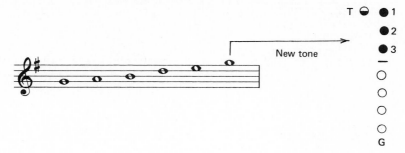

New tone

Play ''Before Dinner.'' Sing with syllables and hand signals.

Before Dinner

Africa

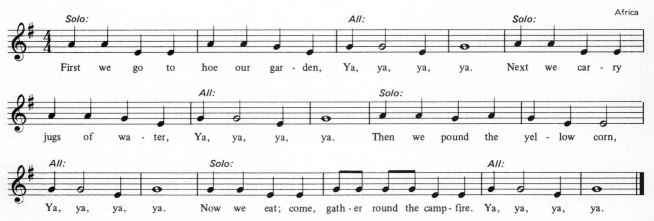

Solo: First we go to hoe our gar - den, *All:* Ya, ya, ya, ya. *Solo:* Next we car - ry jugs of wa - ter, *All:* Ya, ya, ya, ya. *Solo:* Then we pound the yel - low corn, *All:* Ya, ya, ya, ya. *Solo:* Now we eat; come, gath - er round the camp - fire. *All:* Ya, ya, ya, ya.

Edith Lovell Thomas. *The Whole World Singing.* Copyright by Friendship Press. Used by permission.

Sing with a small group on the ''Solo,'' everyone on the ''All.'' A ''call and response'' performed in this manner is called *antiphonal.* Add the last two measures of line one as an ostinato for introduction and coda.

Create additional ostinatos using the tones of the G pentatonic not already used in the song. Improvise or write out.

Play and sing ''Four in a Boat.'' Is this a complete or incomplete G pentatonic scale?

Four in a Boat

Appalachian Mountain Song

1. Four in a boat and the tide rolls high, Four in a boat and the tide rolls high, Four in a boat and the tide rolls high, Wait - ing for a pret - ty one to come by'm by.

2. Choose your partner and stay all day,
   Choose your partner and stay all day,
   Choose your partner and stay all day,
   We don't care what the old folks say.

3. Eight in a boat and it won't go round.
   Eight in a boat and it won't go round,
   Eight in a boat and it won't go round,
   Swing that pretty one you've just found.

Create several ostinatos and perform as introduction, interlude and coda.
Use the recorder, guitar, or piano if possible.

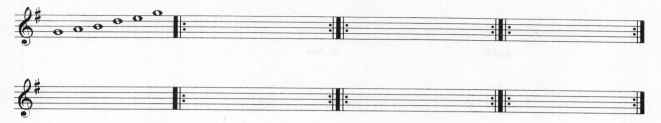

It is very common for the tones of a pentatonic scale to occur both above and below the keynote in the octave from low *sol* to *sol* above *do*.

Improvise a melody using these tones, beginning and ending on G.

Improvise a duet or trio.

Play and sing "All Night, All Day." Note the D.C. al Fine. Is this a complete or incomplete G pentatonic scale? Add ostinatos.

Perform the refrain and the verse in two groups simultaneously. Two songs or two parts of the same song which sound well when performed together are called *partner songs*.

Any pentatonic songs with compatible meters and the same keynote may be partner songs. Write and perform a song that can be performed as a partner to either the "Before Dinner" or "Four in a Boat." Both are G pentatonic.

The F pentatonic scale is:

B♭ may or may not be placed in the key signature. This does not affect the scale. Although a B♭ is not used in F pentatonic, its placement in the key signature does signal a keynote of F.

Perform each of the following songs on recorder. Each is F pentatonic. Then sing with syllables and hand signals. Sing with words. Finally, write and perform ostinatos with voice (add words) and instruments (recorder, guitar, piano, or classroom percussion.)

One of These Days
(Echo Song)

American Folk Song

Ostinatos:

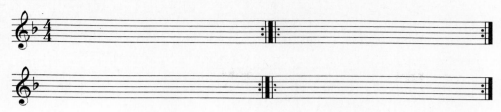

Mr. Rabbit

Folk Song from Southern United States

Verse

1. Mis-ter Rab-bit, Mis-ter Rab-bit, Your ear's might-y long!" "Yes in - deed, they're put on wrong."_
2. Your foot's might-y red!" "Yes in - deed, I'm al -most dead."_

Refrain

Ev - 'ry lit - tle soul must shine, shine, shine._ Ev - 'ry lit - tle soul must shine,_ shine, shine.

3. "Your coat's mighty gray!"
   "Yes indeed, 'twas made that way."
4. "Your tail's mighty white!"
   "Yes indeed, I'm going out of sight."
5. "You hop mighty high!"
   "Yes indeed, up to the sky."

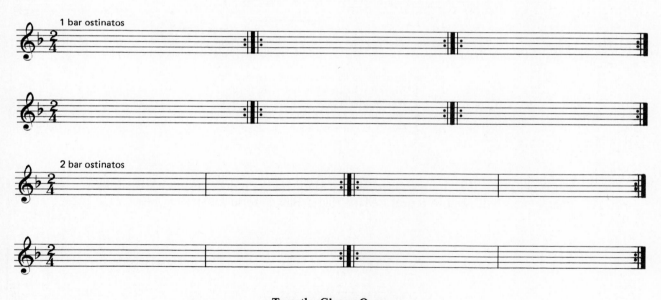

1 bar ostinatos

2 bar ostinatos

Turn the Glasses Over

American Singing Game

I've been to Har - lem, I've been to Do - ver, I've trav -eled this wide world all o - ver,

O - ver, o - ver, three times o - ver, Drink what you have to drink and turn the glass - es o - ver,

123

Sail-ing east, sail-ing west, Sail-ing o-ver the o-cean, Bet-ter watch out when the boat be-gins to rock, or you'll lose your girl in the o-cean.

Ostinatos:

Mary Had a Baby

Spiritual

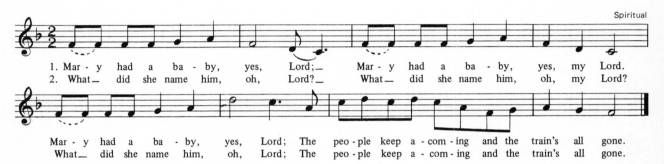

1. Mar-y had a ba-by, yes, Lord;__ Mar-y had a ba-by, yes, my Lord.
2. What__ did she name him, oh, Lord?__ What__ did she name him, oh, my Lord?

Mar-y had a ba-by, yes, Lord; The peo-ple keep a-com-ing and the train's all gone.
What__ did she name him, oh, Lord; The peo-ple keep a-com-ing and the train's all gone.

3. Mary named him Jesus, yes, Lord; etc.
4. Where was he born, oh, Lord? etc.
5. Born in a stable, yes, Lord; etc.
6. Who came to see him, oh, Lord? etc.
7. Shepherds came to see him, yes, Lord, etc.

Perform "Turn the Glasses Over" and "Mary Had a Baby" together as partner songs. You will need to repeat "Mary Had a Baby" to make sixteen measures.

Ostinatos:

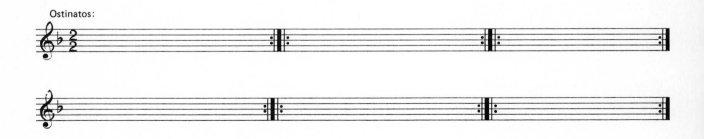

Write a song as a partner to be performed with one of the above in F pentatonic.

D pentatonic is:

d   r   m   s   l   d'

Two sharps are used in the key signature (although only one is used in the scale) to signal D as the keynote.

Swing Low, Sweet Chariot

Spiritual

Swing low, sweet char - i - ot; ___ Com - in' for to car - ry me home!

Swing ___ low, sweet char - i - ot; ___ Com - in' for to car - ry me home. I

looked ov - er Jor - dan, an' what did I see. ___ Com - in' for to car - ry me home! A

band ___ of an - gels com - in' af - ter me; ___ Com - in' for to car - ry me home!

2. If you get there before I do, . . .
   Just tell my friends that I'm a-comin' too, . . .

3. I'm sometimes up an' sometimes down, . . .
   But still my soul feels heavenly bound, . . .

From *Guitar in the Classroom*, 1971, Timmerman and Griffith (Dubuque: William C. Brown)

Play and sing "Swing Low, Sweet Chariot."

Perform "Swing Low, Sweet Chariot" antiphonally as suggested by the call-response (solo-chorus).
   Add ostinatos. (Use instruments if possible.)

Additional pentatonic scales using key signatures already learned are:

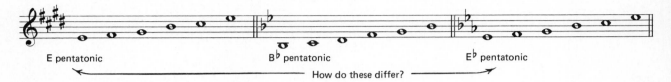

E pentatonic   B♭ pentatonic   E♭ pentatonic

←————————————— How do these differ? —————————————→

Self-checking Chapter Review

Complete the following crossword puzzle.

Across

1. five–toned scale
6.
7.
8. relative minor of C
9. anti _____
11. theme and _____
13. very soft
14.

Down

1. pianissimo
2. type of song with 2 parts
3. number in a duet
4. repeated pattern
5.
6. What G is if C is *do*.
9. soft
10. theme _____ variation
12.
13. piano

Melody	*intervals ~ arpeggio ~ monophony*
Harmony	*polyphony ~ homophony*
Timbre	*legato/staccato ~ SATB ~ strings ~ brass ~ woodwinds ~ percussion*
Form	*ternary*

Play and sing ''Listen While My Flute is Playing.''

Listen While My Flute is Playing

Scale Song

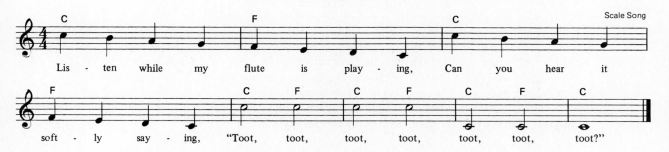

Lis - ten while my flute is play - ing, Can you hear it

soft - ly say - ing, "Toot, toot, toot, toot, toot, toot, toot?"

What is the highest note? The lowest?

   The range of the song is one *octave* (or eight pitch names). The octave is a basic *interval* (distance between two pitches) in music.

The numerical value of any interval is found by counting the pitch names from one tone to the next.

```
C  D  E  F  G  A  B  C
1  2  3  4  5  6  7  8
```

Do not worry about sharps or flats in between, since this does not affect the numerical value of an interval; that is, C to C′ is always an octave.

   Another way to determine the numerical value of an interval is to count lines and spaces, taking care to begin on the first pitch and end on the final one.

What is the distance between C and G? (C D E F G = fifth)

Between C and E? C and F? C and B?

Identify the numerical value of each of the following intervals.

Write a note that gives the correct numerical value of the indicated interval *above* the given note.

6th   4th   8va   3rd

Write a note that gives the correct numerical value of the indicated interval *below* the given note.

8va   5th   7th   2nd   4th

Intervals that are smaller than an octave are called *simple* intervals. All of those above are simple intervals. Intervals that are larger than an octave are called *compound* intervals.

Identify the numerical value of each of the following:

Write a note that gives the correct numerical value of the indicated interval *above* the given note.

10th   12th   9th   11th

Write a note that gives the correct numerical value of the indicated interval *below* the given note.

4th   10th   9th   8va

Which are simple? Compound?

Play and sing "Make New Friends." Accompany with an F major chord.

Make New Friends

Make new friends but keep— the— old,— One is sil - ver and the oth - er gold.

What is the interval between:

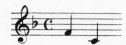

How many half-steps in this interval? A fourth with five half-steps (or two and a half steps) is called a *perfect* fourth.

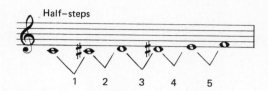

The term "fourth" describes the numerical value of this interval, while "perfect" describes its *quality*. All intervals may be designated by both a numerical and qualitative label. The numerical label is general, but "perfect" describes the specific effect or quality. A perfect interval is consider "pure" acoustically and has been traditionally labeled as "perfect." Only unisons, fourths, fifths and octaves may be perfect. The following are labels, both numerically and qualitatively, of intervals smaller than the perfect fourth.

Sing and play each. Find examples in "Make New Friends." Which interval cannot be found?

Write these intervals (above):

Play and sing.

Write these intervals (above):

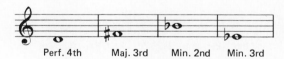

Play and sing.

Write these intervals (below):

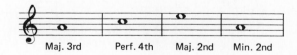

Play and sing.

Identify these intervals.

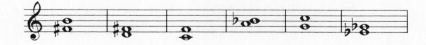

Play and sing "Dona Nobis Pacem." There are many wide intervals in this song.

Dona Nobis Pacem

Intervals wider than a perfect fourth include:

Aug. 4th	Perf. 5th	Min. 6th	Maj. 6th	Min. 7th	Maj. 7th	Perf. 8va
(3 steps)	(3½ steps)	(4 steps)	(4½ steps)	(5 steps)	(5½ steps)	(6 steps)

Play and sing each of these.

Find examples in "Dona Nobis Pacem." Which intervals do not occur?

Write these intervals (above):

Perf. 5th   Min. 6th   Aug. 4th   Maj. 7th   Perf. 8va   Min. 7th

Play and sing.
    Write these intervals (above):

Min. 6th   Perf. 5th   Min. 7th   Perf. 8va   Aug. 4th   Maj. 7th

Play and sing. Write these intervals (below):

Min. 7th   Perf. 5th   Perf. 8va   Maj. 6th   Min. 6th

Play and sing.
    Write these intervals (above):

Min. 2nd   Perf. 5th   Perf. 4th   Min. 7th   Maj. 3rd   Maj. 6th

Play and sing.
Identify these intervals.

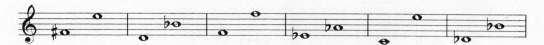

Play both "Make New Friends" and "Dona Nobis Pacem" without accompaniment. This creates a type of musical texture called *monophonic*. There is only melody in a monophonic texture, no harmony. *Monophony* may be created by a solo voice, several voices in unison, a solo instrument, several instruments in unison, or a combination of voices and instruments as long as there is only a *unison* melody. (The presence of non-pitched rhythm instruments will not alter this.)

monophony

Sing or play "Make New Friends" as a two-part round. Play or sing "Dona Nobis Pacem" as a three-part round. This texture is *polyphonic*.

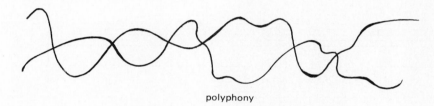

polyphony

Polyphony produces harmony because different melodies are occurring at the same time (or different phrases of the same melody, as with a round).

Listen to

On the Steppes of Central Asia by Borodin (1833–1887)
(Bowmar Orchestral Library No. 78)

Two themes are introduced separately at the beginning of the composition and then played together near the end, thus creating a polyphonic composition. Which instruments play each theme? How is it possible to hear both themes during the polyphony?

"ON THE STEPPES OF CENTRAL ASIA" from The Bowmar Orchestral Library "Musical Kaleidoscope" (No. 093) by: Lucille Wood Copyright ©1967 by Bowmar Noble, a division of Belwin–Mills Publishing Corp. Used With Permission All Rights Reserved.

Play and sing "All Through the Night" with the descant.

All Through the Night

From *Growing with Music,* Wilson et al., Book 5 (Englewood Cliffs, NJ: Prentice–Hall, Inc., 1966)

This, too, is an example of polyphony. Notice there are four phrases in an AABA form. This is known as three-part or ternary form. (ABA is its simplest form.) Ternary form is very common in music. It may occur as ABA, AABA, AABBA, etc.

Listen to

Minuet by Mozart (1756–1791)
(Bowmar Orchestral Library No. 53)

The theme of A is:

The theme of B is:

Listen particularly for the return of the A theme in this ABA (ternary) form.

A third type of texture is called *homophonic*. Homophony means one melody is accompanied by chords.

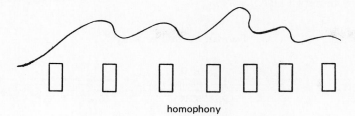

homophony

Play and sing "Drum and Fiddle" adding the C and G chord on guitar or auto-harp. This is an example of homophony.

Drum and Fiddle

Traditional

Boom, boom goes the drum, And a hi did-dle did-dle goes the fid-dle; And a

hi did-dle did-dle did-dle did-dle did-dle dum Goes the fid-dle fid-dle fid-dle fid-dle

fid-dle fid-dle fum; Goes the fid-dle and the big bass drum. Boom, boom goes the drum.

From *Growing with Music,* Wilson et al., Book 3 (Englewood Cliffs, NJ: Prentice–Hall, Inc., 1966)

Sing "Make New Friends" again as you accompany on the guitar or piano. Use F major chord throughout. Play the piano chord like this:

etc.

When the tones of a chord are broken like this, it is called an *arpeggio*. Accompanying with an arpeggio does not change the texture. This is still homophonic since the tones of the arpeggio do not create a second, independent melody. Try this arpeggio to "Make New Friends" on the piano.

etc.

Improvise an arpeggio that is compatible in $\frac{4}{4}$ and add to the song.

Chords may be arpeggiated on the guitar too.

Play the F major chord on the guitar this way to provide accompaniment.

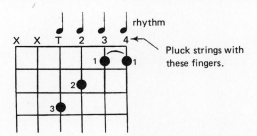

rhythm

X X T 2 3 4

Pluck strings with these fingers.

Arpeggios must fit the meter and accent of a given key, in this case, $\frac{4}{4}$. Experiment with other chords in this manner.

Play and sing and accompany (homophonically) the "German Instrument Song." This is ternary (ABA). Why?

German Instrument Song

English Words by Margaret Marks

German Folk Song

1. If I had a fid - dle, fid - dle, fid - dle, If I had a fid - dle, how I'd play! Fid - dle - dee and fid - dle day, One, two, three, four hours a day! If I had a fid - dle, fid - dle, fid - dle, If I had a fid - dle, how I'd play!

2. If I had a flute, a flute, a flute, oh, If I had a flute, oh, how I'd play! Too - dle - dee and too - dle day, One, two, three, four hours a day! If I had a flute, a flute, a flute, oh, If I had a flute, oh, how I'd play!

3. If I had a cello, cello, cello. . .
Zum, zum, zum and zum, zum, zay. . .

4. If I had a trumpet, trumpet, trumpet. . .
Toot, toot, toot and toot, toot, tay. . .

5. If I had a trombone, trombone, trombone. . .
Pum, pum, pum and pum, pum, pay. . .

6. If I had a drum, a drum, a drum. . .
Boom, boom, boom and a boom, boom, bay. . .

From MAKING MUSIC YOUR OWN 3. ©1971 General Learning Corporation. Reprinted by permission of Silver Burdett Company.

Human voices are classified by range and quality as *soprano, alto, tenor* and *bass* (SATB).

The soprano voice is the highest and brightest female voice. Its range is approximately:

The alto is lower and darker, with this approximate range:

The tenor voice is the male counterpart of the soprano. The approximate tenor range is:

The bass voice is the lowest and darkest male voice with an approximate range of:

134

These are the four basic designations for voice types. Two intermediary vocal types are sometimes used, the *mezzo* (medium) *soprano,* and the *baritone,* which are types respectively between the soprano–alto and tenor–bass ranges. Although soprano and alto parts are usually sung by females, there are boy sopranos and altos. There are sometimes even female tenors and basses.

Play and sing "The Orchestra" without accompaniment. This is an example of monophony.

Accompany with the C and G[7] as indicated with the melody in unison. This is an example of homophony. (Can you make an arpeggiated accompaniment?)

Divide into five sections, each group playing or singing its respective part. (You may need a conductor). This is an example of polyphony. Note the chord progressions in each section are identical: C G[7] G[7] C C G[7] G[7] C. This is why the five different melodies work well together harmonically. They all have an identical chord structure.

The instruments of a symphony orchestra are divided into four sections. The *string* family is the violin family, consisting, from high to low, of:

*Photos by Donald Smith,
Slide City, Tucson, Arizona.*

Violin

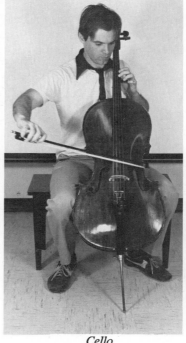

Cello

Bass

All have four strings and may be both bowed or plucked (*pizzicato*). Members of the violin family can play very smooth melodies, a style called *legato,* when played with the bow. Plucked strings are very detached, a style called *staccato.*

Tuba   *Trombone*

Flugel horn   *French horn*   *Trumpet*

Most brass instruments have valves, with the exception of the trombone which has a moveable slide. The action of the lips and the breath pressure *plus* the valves (or slide) enable the performer to change pitches.

Instruments of the woodwind family are quite diverse. Some have reeds, some do not. Reeds are considered single when one piece of cane is attached to a mouthpiece and set into vibration. Double reeds form their own mouthpiece, the player actually blowing through two attached pieces of cane. All woodwind instruments finger in a similar manner, following patterns which are akin to the recorder.

Below are the most common woodwind instruments:

Alto saxophone   Clarinet

Flute   Piccolo

*Photos by Donald Smith,
Slide City, Tucson, Arizona.*

Bassoon   Oboe

The last family is the percussion. These are the most diverse of all. Some have no definite pitch, others do. Some are shaken, other struck. Among these are:

Indefinite	Definite pitch
snare drum	timpani (kettle drums)
bass drum	glockenspiel
triangle	marimba
cymbals	tubular chimes
cowbell	vibraharp
tambourine	xylophone
sleigh bells	celesta

Photo by Donald Smith,
Slide City, Tucson, Arizona.

Snare drum   *Xylophone*

In addition, there are other instruments which do not clearly belong in any one of these four orchestral families because they are not primarily orchestral instruments. These include the harp, piano, organ, and harpsichord.

Electronic music is frequently created on a recently invented instrument, the synthesizer.

Listen to

The Young Person's Guide to the Orchestra by Britten (1913–1976)
(Bowmar Orchestral Library No. 83)

Britten uses various sections and instruments of the orchestra to provide variations on a theme by the older composer, Purcell.

"YOUNG PERSON'S GUIDE TO THE ORCHESTRA" from The Bowmar Orchestral Library "Ensembles, Large and Small" (No. 098) Copyright ©1967 by Bowmar Noble, a division of Belwin–Mills Publishing Corp. Used With Permission. All Rights Reserved.

Listen and observe the sequence in which each of the following sections and instruments of the entire orchestra is heard.

full orchestra	violins
woodwind family	viola
brass family	cellos
string family	double bass
percussion family	harp
full orchestra	french horns
	trumpets
flutes and piccolo	trombone and tuba
two oboes	percussion
two clarinets	
bassoons	full orchestra

138

Play, sing and accompany "We Are Good Musicians." Add additional verses about the instruments just discussed and heard.

We Are Good Musicians

German Folk Song

Fast

We are good mu - si - cians, we sing and play each day.
We are good mu - si - cians, now hear us as we play.

1. I can play the bass drum,
2. I can play the song bell,

hear him play the bass drum: boom, boom, boom, boom, boom, boom, boom, boom boom - ty boom, boom boom!
hear (her) play the song bell: *(play the song bell)*

3. I can play the wood block,
   Hear him play the wood block:
   (Play the wood block)

4. I can play the triangle,
   Hear him play the triangle:
   (Play the triangle)

Self-checking Chapter Review

Identify these intervals by *numerical* value.

1 ___ 2 ___ 3 ___ 4 ___ 5 ___ 6 ___ 7 ___ 8 ___ 9 ___ 10 ___

11. Which are compound? ___

Identify these intervals by *quality* and *numerical* value.

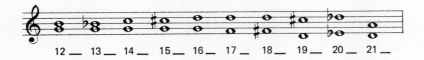

12 ___ 13 ___ 14 ___ 15 ___ 16 ___ 17 ___ 18 ___ 19 ___ 20 ___ 21 ___

Match column II to column I.

1. ___ monophony	A.	mezzo
2. ___ polyphony	B.	high female voice
3. ___ homophony	C.	two or more independent melodies
4. ___ ternary	D.	smooth
5. ___ soprano	E.	single and double reeds
6. ___ alto	F.	detached
7. ___ tenor	G.	unison
8. ___ bass	H.	high male voice
9. ___ medium soprano	I.	valves and slides
10. ___ strings	J.	melody plus harmony
11. ___ woodwinds	K.	violins and cellos
12. ___ brass	L.	definite and indefinite pitch
13. ___ percussion	M.	ABA
14. ___ pizzicato	N.	plucked
15. ___ legato	O.	low female voice
16. ___ staccato	P.	low male voice

139

Find these instruments in the "word find" below. Answers may appear horizontal, vertical or diagonal, forward or backward.

piccolo	violin	triangle
flute	viola	saxophone
alto flute	cello	bells
clarinet	bass	harp
oboe	chimes	bow
bassoon	timpani[1]	piano
french horn	snare drum	organ
trombone	cymbals	moog[2]
tuba	celesta	

```
T E T B O W Z S R V I O L I N
I T E T U L F V O L O C C I P
M U K R Y I R J P W P Q A P K
P L N I H T E N I R A L C J M
A F A A X Y N T A U A N O B N
N O G N Z L C B N G M H A A I
I T R G F C H L O K L S S S S
U L O L D C H I M E S S A S L
B A B E E E O T A N R H X O A
A E J L E L R A U O O V O O B
G V L X X E N Q Y B Z I P N M
C O W L F S G T O M A O H L Y
H I O F S T V E B O C L O Q C
E E D M G A W U M R P A N D O
S N A R E D R U M T N O E R S
```

[1]also spelled timpanii

[2]a type of synthesizer

Melody   *major diatonic scale ~ heptatonic ~ non-harmonic tones*
Harmony   *tonic triad ~ subdominant triad ~ dominant chord ~*
              harmonizing songs ~ root position ~ inversions ~
              circle of fifths
Form   *binary*

A scale, as seen earlier, is a catalog of pitches used in a song. The chromatic scale uses twelve tones whereas the pentatonic has only five. In Western (European-based) music, one of the most common scales is the *major diatonic*.

Play and sing ''Chester.''

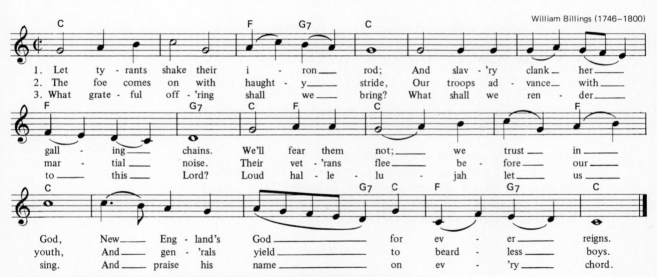

Chester

William Billings (1746–1800)

1. Let ty - rants shake their i - ron rod; And slav - 'ry clank her
2. The foe comes on with haught - y stride, Our troops ad - vance with
3. What grate - ful off - 'ring shall we bring? What shall we ren - der

gall - ing chains. We'll fear them not; we trust in
mar - tial noise. Their vet - 'rans flee be - fore our
to this Lord? Loud hal - le - lu - jah let us

God, New Eng - land's God for ev - er reigns.
youth, And gen - 'rals yield to beard - less boys.
sing. And praise his name on ev - 'ry chord.

From The Birchard Music Series Book 5. ©1962. Used by permission of Summy–Birchard Music.

If the notes used in ''Chester'' are placed on a staff in the order in which they occur, the results are:

Arranged from low to high, this scale is:

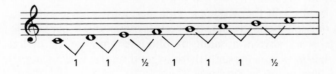

1   1   ½   1   1   1   ½

This scale is seven-toned (*heptatonic*) and uses, in order, each pitch name in the musical alphabet.

C D E F G A B C'

This is typical of a *diatonic* scale. In addition, a diatonic scale has two half-steps and five whole-steps. The scale is *major* because the half-steps occur *always* between the third–fourth and seventh–eighth tones. C major is the only major scale using no sharps or flats.

How does C major differ from C pentatonic? Both include the same five notes, but C major has two additional tones, *fa* (4th tone) and *ti* (7th tone).

Both of these are tendency tones because they form half steps with other tones. *Fa* has a tendency to pull to *mi* and *ti* to high *do*. The hand signals for these two tones are:

These show the downward tendency of *fa* (to *mi*) and the upward tendency of *ti* (to *do'*).

Sing "Chester," using syllables and hand signals.

Listen to

"Chester" from the *New England Triptych* by William Schuman (1910–   )
(Bowmar Orchestral Library No. 75)

How is unity achieved in this work? Variety?

Improvise a melody using the C major scale. Be certain the tendency of *fa* and *ti* is observed. Begin and end on C (low or high).

Sing and play "Lullaby," performing as a round. Crescendo when the melody ascends. Decrescendo when the melody descends.

Like the C pentatonic, not all notes of the C major scale need be used in a melody. The rest may be used in the accompanying harmony.

How can one tell the difference between C major and C pentatonic if some notes are missing? It is not always possible by purely examining the melody. Generally, however, if either *fa* or *ti* is present, there is good reason to consider the song major. If both are present, there is no doubt.

Play and sing "Kum Ba Yah." Is this major or pentatonic? Why?

Kum - Ba - Yah

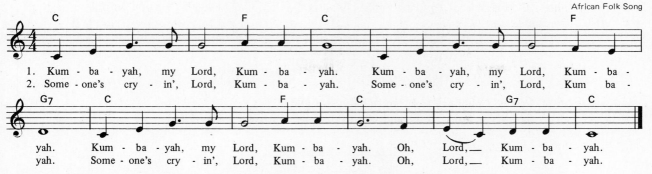

African Folk Song

1. Kum - ba - yah, my Lord, Kum - ba - yah. Kum - ba - yah, my Lord, Kum - ba -
2. Some - one's cry - in', Lord, Kum - ba - yah. Some - one's cry - in', Lord, Kum ba -

yah. Kum - ba - yah, my Lord, Kum - ba - yah. Oh, Lord,__ Kum - ba - yah.
yah. Some - one's cry - in', Lord, Kum - ba - yah. Oh, Lord,__ Kum - ba - yah.

From *Music Fundamentals*, by Vito Puopalo, New York: Schirmer Books, a division of Macmillan Publishing Co., Inc. 1976. Used by permission.

Many songs may be accompanied by three (or fewer) chords. The chords are derived from the major scale.

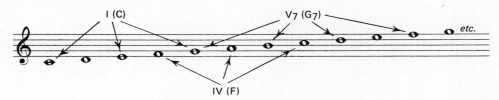

A triad is a chord with three pitches, each separated by the interval of a third. A triad consists of *root, third,* and *fifth.*

The triad built on *do* is called the *tonic triad* (I). It consists of *do-mi-sol. Do* is the root of the chord, *mi* is the third, and *sol* the fifth.

This may also be called the C major triad (or chord) since the key is C. This is probably the most important chord in the entire song since it stabilizes the tonality. Most songs end on the I chord.

The chord built on the fourth note of the scale is called the *subdominant triad* (IV). It consists of *fa-la-do'. Fa* is the root, *la* the third, and *do'* the fifth.

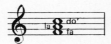

This may also be called the F major triad or chord.

The chord built on the fifth note of the scale is called the *dominant triad* (V). It consists of *sol-ti-re'. Sol* is the root, *ti* the third, and *re'* the fifth. It may be called the G major triad or chord.

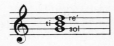

Most frequently, a fourth tone is added to the dominant chord to provide dissonance. *"Ti"* provides one tendency tone, but the addition of *"fa"* (F in this case) to the basic

143

triad adds tension to the chord. Since *fa* is the interval of a 7th (seven pitch names) above the chord root, *sol,* the chord is called the dominant seventh (V₇), or, in this particular case, G₇.

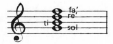

Practice playing, C,F, and G₇ on the guitar.
Practice playing C,F, and G₇ on the piano in root position.

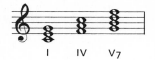

Notice how G₇ (V₇) leads back to the tonic (I) chord.

Improvise with these chord progressions using even, uneven and syncopated patterns. Begin and end on the tonic triad.

Play and sing "Michael Row the Boat Ashore." Provide harmony as indicated on the piano, guitar, or Autoharp. Notice how the song both begins and ends on the tonic (I) chord—C major.

Michael, Row the Boat Ashore

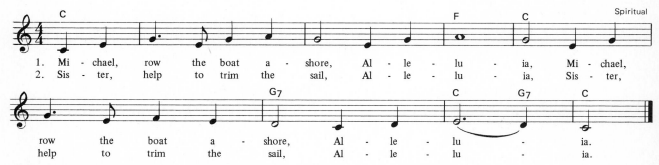

From *Music Fundamentals,* by Vito Puopalo. New York: Schirmer Books, a division of Macmillan Publishing Co., Inc. 1976. Used by permission.

When a melody is provided without harmony, chords can be determined by the following:

1. Determine the key and scale of the song.
2. Determine the I, IV and V₇ chords in this key.
3. Decide how often a chord is needed in the song.

    $\frac{2}{4}$ usually once in a bar 𝅗𝅥, possibly twice 𝅘𝅥 𝅘𝅥
    $\frac{3}{4}$ usually once in a bar 𝅗𝅥., possibly three times 𝅘𝅥 𝅘𝅥 𝅘𝅥
    $\frac{4}{4}$ usually once in a bar 𝅝 or twice in a bar 𝅗𝅥 𝅗𝅥, rarely four times in a bar 𝅘𝅥 𝅘𝅥 𝅘𝅥 𝅘𝅥
    $\frac{6}{8}$ usually once in a bar 𝅗𝅥. or twice 𝅗𝅥. 𝅗𝅥.

4. Each unit, according to No. 3, is analyzed to see into which chord the majority of the melody pitches fit. (Remember: the song *must* end on I and *often* begin on I.) Keep these points in mind:
    a. An anacrusis is rarely harmonized.
    b. The hierarchy for selecting chords is I, V₇ and then IV.

Sing and Play

Shuckin' of the Corn

Folk Song from Tennessee

Verse

1. I have a ship on the o - cean,___ All lin'd with sil - ver and gold,___ Be -
2. The wind blows cold in ___ Cai - ro, ___ The sun re - fus - es to shine, ___ Be -

fore I'd see my true love suf - fer, that ship 'ud be an - chored and sold.___
fore I'd see my true love suf - fer, I'd work all the sum - mer time. ___

Refrain

I'm a - go - in' to the shuck - in' of the corn,___ I'm a - go - in' to the

shuck - in' of the corn, ___ A shuck - in' of the corn and a -

blow - in' of the horn, I'm a - go - in' to the shuck - in' of the corn. ___

Harmonize "Shuckin' of the Corn." For $\frac{2}{4}$, use s as the basis of chord selection. (One chord per measure.)

The chords are:

I	IV	V7
CEG	FAC	GBDF

First line

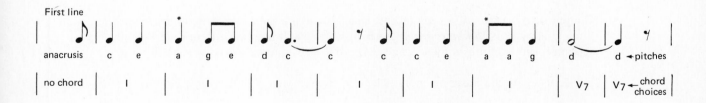

| anacrusis | c | e | a | g | e | d c | c | | c | c | e | a | g | d | d ← pitches |
| no chord | I | | I | | I | | I | | | I | | I | | V7 | V7 ← chord choices |

Non-harmonic tones are those which do not belong in the chord. Harmonic or chordal tones should always outnumber the non-harmonic.

Complete the harmony.

It is well to keep the harmony as simple as possible and to sing with the accompaniment to see if it indeed is effective. Many people can quickly learn to harmonize a song "by ear" using the *primary chords* (I, IV, and V₇). Composers and arrangers who desire richer harmony often utilize chords built on the second, third, or sixth degrees of the scale. These chords are called *secondary* triads and they do provide harmonic variety. The primary triads, however, provide a basic accompaniment and suffice very nicely.

Harmonize "An April Day."

An April Day

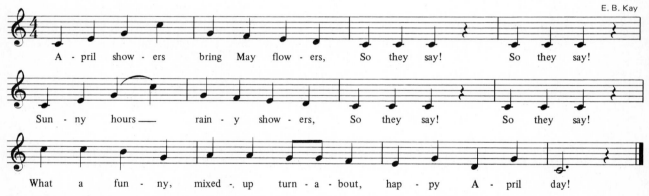

If a phrase or section of a song repeats exactly, use the same harmony on the repetition. This piece is in *binary form* (AAB by phrases). It has two different phrases or sections. Binary form is most simply AB, but also may be AAB or AABB.

For $\frac{4}{4}$, use s as the basis of chord selection (two chords per measure).

Line one ┃   ┃   ┃   ┃   ┃

Line two ┃   ┃   ┃   ┃   ┃

Line three ┃   ┃   ┃   ‖

A guitar chord is fingered so all tones strummed are within the given chord.

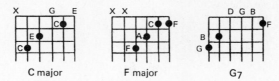

On the piano, chord inversions are frequently used to allow smoother voice leading between chords. A chord *inversion* is one in which the same tones are used, but the root is *not* the lowest tone. If played by the right hand in root position, the I, IV and V7 chords of C major are:

The root, however, can be played in the left hand and a chord inversion used in the right.

The tonic is most frequently kept in root position.

The subdominant is used in second inversion. (The fifth of the chord is the lowest sounding tone.)

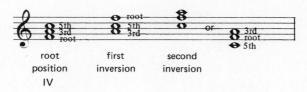

The dominant seventh is used in first inversion. The third of the chord is the lowest sounding tone. Frequently, *re,* a non-essential tone is eliminated in the V_7 to maintain three tones only in the chord.

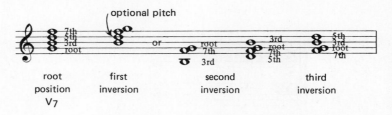

Thus, the positions for the I, IV, and V_7 chords for the right hand (with roots provided by the left hand) are

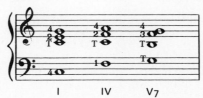

Practice these chord patterns in $\frac{2}{4}$, $\frac{3}{4}$, $\frac{4}{4}$, $\frac{6}{8}$. Try accompanying all C major songs in this chapter using these chords.

Play and sing "My Pony."

My Pony

Trot, trot, trot! Trot, my po - ny, trot. Where it's smooth and where it's ston - y, Trot a - long my lit - tle po - ny, Go and nev - er stop! Trot, my po - ny, trot!

Eunice Boardman and Beth Landis, *Exploratory Music 1*, 1966. Holt Rinehart and Winston, Inc. Reprinted by permission.

The key is G major. Why?

1   1   ½   1   1   1   ½

A sharp is needed on F to provide a whole step between *la–ti* (E–F♯) and half-step between *ti–do'* (F♯–G).

Harmony is added to "My Pony" by first determining the primary triads in G major, and then harmonizing each bar (♩), always ending on G (and trying to begin on it as well).

Sing and accompany "My Pony" on guitar.

Piano chords in G major are:

Add a piano accompaniment (root-chord) to "My Pony."

Play, sing and accompany "East Side, West Side."

East Side, West Side

Charles B. Lawler

James W. Blake

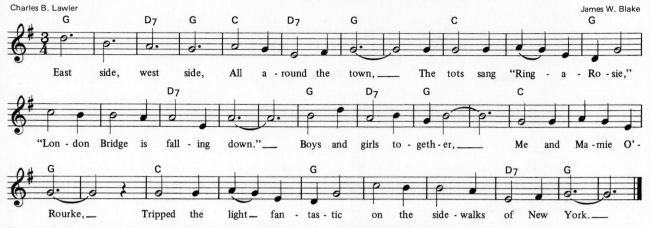

East side, west side, All a-round the town,___ The tots sang "Ring - a - Ro-sie," "Lon - don Bridge is fall - ing down."___ Boys and girls to - geth - er,___ Me and Ma - mie O'- Rourke,___ Tripped the light fan - tas - tic on the side - walks of New York.___

From *Music Fundamentals* by Vito Puopalo, New York: Schirmer Books, a Division of Macmillan Publishing Co., Inc. 1976. Used by permission.

Harmonize, play, sing, and accompany "The Wabash Cannon Ball."

The Wabash Cannon Ball

American

From the broad At - lan - tic O - cean to the far Pa - cif - ic shore, On the plains and in the moun - tains you can hear her en - gines roar. She's long, tall, dark, and hand - some, she's loved by one and all, She's a mo - dern lo - co - mo - tive called the Wa - bash Can - non Ball.

2. Hear the moaning of her whistle and the rhythm of her roar
As she races over hill and plain and goes from shore to shore,
As she skims through mighty cities, they hail her one and all,
She's the pride of our entire land, the Wabash Cannon Ball.

3. Now, the eastern states are wonderful, so the western people say,
From New York to old St. Louis and Chicago by the way,
Through the hills of Minnesota where the rippling waters fall,
The finest way to travel's on the Wabash Cannon Ball.

For $\frac{2}{2}$, use o or ♩ as the basis of chord selection.

Play and sing "This Land is Your Land."

This Land is Your Land

Words and Music by
Woody Guthrie (1912–1967)

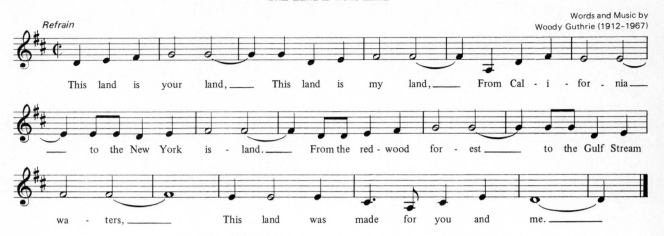

This land is your land,____ This land is my land,____ From Cal - i - for - nia____

____ to the New York is - land.____ From the red - wood for - est____ to the Gulf Stream

wa - ters,____ This land was made for you and me.____

Verses (same melody as refrain)

1. As I was walking that ribbon of highway I saw above me that endless skyway,
   I saw below me that golden valley, This land was made for you and me.
2. I've roamed and rambled and followed my footsteps to the sparkling sands of
   her diamond deserts,
   And all around me a voice was sounding, This land was made for you and me.
3. When the sun comes shining and I was strolling and the wheat fields waving and
   the dust clouds rolling,
   As the fog was lifting a voice was chanting, This land was made for you and me.

The key of "This Land is Your Land" is D major. C♯ and F♯ are needed in the key signature to provide the necessary half-step and whole-step relationships in the scale.

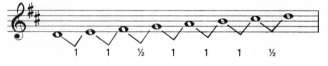

The primary triads in root position are:

In inversion, these chords are:

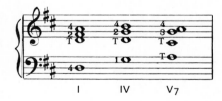

Accompany "This Land is Your Land" on guitar, Autoharp, and piano.
Harmonize, sing, play, and accompany "Sweet Betsy from Pike."

Sweet Betsy from Pike

U.S. Folk Song

1. Did you ev - er hear of sweet Bet - sy from Pike, Who crossed the wide
2. The al - ka - li des - ert was burn - ing and bare, And Ike cried in

prai - rie with her hus - band, Ike, With two yoke of cat - tle and
fear, "We are lost, I de - clare! My dear old Pike Coun - ty I'll

one spot - ted hog, A tall Shang - hai roost - er, and an old yal - ler dog?
go back to you." Said Bet - sy, "You'll go by your - self if you do."

Refrain

Sing_ too ra li oo ra li oo ra li ay, Sing_ too ra li oo ra li oo ra li ay.

3. They swam the wide rivers and crossed the tall peaks.
They camped on the prairie for weeks and for weeks;
They fought off the Indians with musket and ball,
And reached California in spite of it all. *(Refrain)*

For $\frac{3}{4}$, use $\dotted{\half}$ as the basis of chord selection.

Harmonize, sing, play, and accompany "Pease Porridge Hot."

Pease Porridge Hot

Traditional

Pease por - ridge hot, Pease por - ridge cold, Pease por - ridge in the pot Nine days old.
Some like it hot, Some like it cold, Some like it in the pot Nine days old.

For $\frac{4}{4}$, use $\half$ as the basis for chord selection (two per measure).

$\frac{4}{4}$

In keys using sharps in the signature, the *do* of the major scale is found by calling the last sharp (last on the far right) *ti* and counting up a half-step to *do'*.

Memorize:

It gives you the position of sharps for all six sharp keys. Do you see why?

Play each of the following scales on the recorder.

Play these chords on piano, roots in the left hand, and inversions in the right.

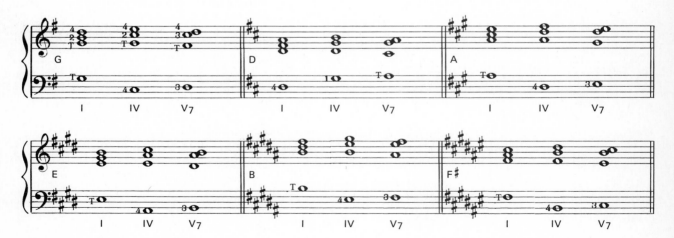

In general, chord inversions for piano playing follow this formula.

sol ——→ la	(1 step up)		sol ——→ sol	(same)
mi ——→ fa	(½ step up)		mi ——→ fa	(½ step up)
do ——→ do	(same)		do ——→ ti	(½ step down)
I	**IV**		**I**	**V₇**

This is true whether the key is C major, or has sharps or flats. Improvise chord progressions on the piano using the above formula. Try various meters and patterns. Begin and end on the I chord.

Play and sing "J'ai Perdu Le Do."

J'ai Perdu Le Do

French

J'ai per - du le do de ma clar - i - ne - te,
I have lost the do on my clar - i - net, oh,
J'ai per - du le do de ma clar - i -
I have lost the do on my clar - i -

net - te. Ah, si Pa - pa sa - vait ça, tra la la! Ah, si Pa - pa sa - vait
net, oh, Ah, if Pa - pa on - ly knew! Tra la la! Ah, if Pa - pa on ly

ça, tra la la! Au pas, ca - ma - rade, au pas, ca - ma - rade, Au pas, au pas, au
knew! Tra la la! March on, tra la la, march on, tra la la, keep step and sing our

pas! Au pas, ca - ma - rade, au pas, ca - ma - rade, Au pas, au pas, au pas!
song! March on, tra la la, march on, tra la la, keep step and march a - long!

The key is F major. B♭ is necessary in the key signature to provide the necessary half and whole step relationships.

The primary chords in root position are:

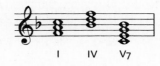

In inversion:

Guitar chords are:

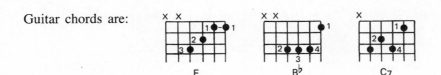

Accompany on the piano and guitar.

Play, sing, and accompany each of the next songs.

I Saw Three Ships

English Carol

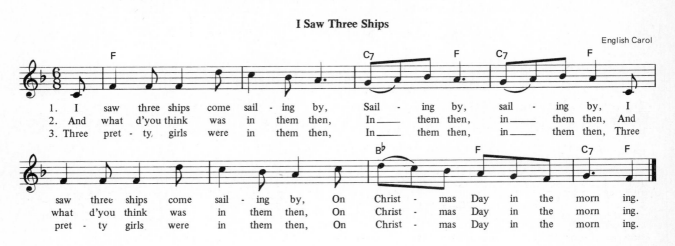

1. I saw three ships come sail - ing by, Sail - ing by, sail - ing by, I
2. And what d'you think was in them then, In them then, in them then, And
3. Three pret - ty girls were in them then, In them then, in them then, Three

saw three ships come sail - ing by, On Christ - mas Day in the morn ing.
what d'you think was in them then, On Christ - mas Day in the morn ing.
pret - ty girls were in them then, On Christ - mas Day in the morn ing.

My Farm

Argentinian Folk Song

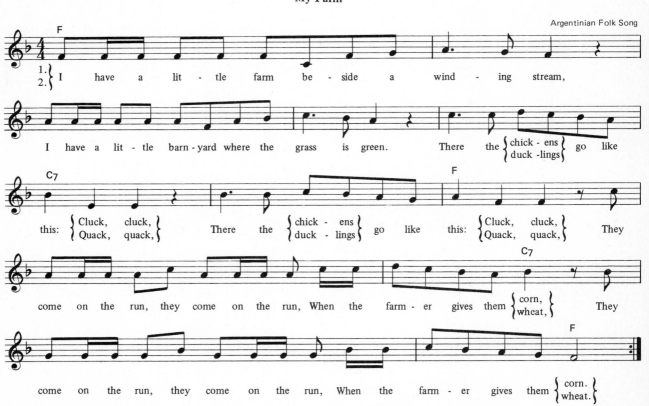

I have a lit - tle farm be - side a wind - ing stream,

I have a lit - tle barn - yard where the grass is green. There the {chick - ens / duck - lings} go like

this: {Cluck, cluck, / Quack, quack,} There the {chick - ens / duck - lings} go like this: {Cluck, cluck, / Quack, quack,} They

come on the run, they come on the run, When the farm - er gives them {corn, / wheat,} They

come on the run, they come on the run, When the farm - er gives them {corn. / wheat.}

3. There the horses go like this:
   Neigh, neigh.
   They come on the run
   When the farmer gives then oats.

4. There the donkeys go like this:
   Hee–haw.
   They come on the run
   When the farmer gives them hay.

154

5. There the piglets go like this:
   Oink–oink.
   They come on the run
   When the farmer gives them whey.

6. There the puppies go like this:
   Woof, woof.
   They come on the run
   When the farmer gives them bones.

7. There the kittens go like this:
   Meow, meow.
   They come on the run
   When the farmer gives them milk.

8. There the milk–cows go like this:
   Moo, moo.
   They come on the run
   When the farmer gives them hay.

From MUSIC NOW AND LONG AGO. Copyright 1956, 1962. Silver Burdett Company. Reprinted by permission.

Harmonize, play, sing, and accompany "Pussy Cat, Pussy Cat."

Pussy Cat, Pussy Cat

J.W. Elliott

Pus - sy cat, pus - sy cat, where have you been? I've been to Lon - don to vis - it the queen.

Pus - sy cat, pus - sy cat, what did you there? I fright - ened a lit - tle mouse un - der her chair.

Eunice Boardman and Beth Landis, *Exploring Music 1*, 1966. Holt, Rinehart and Winston, Inc. Reprinted by permission.

For $\frac{6}{8}$, use ♩. as the basis for chord selection (two per measure)
Play and sing "Oh, Give Thanks."

Oh, Give Thanks

French Round

Oh, give thanks, Oh, give thanks, Oh, give thanks un - to the Lord, for He is

gra - cious and His mer - cy en - dur - eth, en - dur - eth for - ev - er.

From *Growing With Music*, Wilson et al., Book 5 (Englewood Cliffs, NJ: Prentice–Hall, Inc., 1966)

The key is B♭ major. B♭ and E♭ are necessary in the key signature to provide the necessary half and whole step relationships.

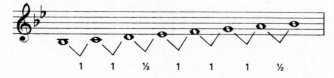

1   1   ½   1   1   1   ½

The primary chords in root position are:

In inversion: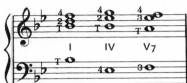

The capo is used on the guitar to transpose to higher keys. The elastic or clamping device attaches around the neck and shortens all strings the same length. The capo is treated like the end of the string (nut). Chords played relative to this produce keys a half-step higher for each fret the capo covers. Photo by Donald Smith, Slide City, Tucson, Arizona.

For guitar chords, place a capo on the first fret and use A, D, and E_7 as the primary chords, one fret higher than normally. The capo on the first fret has the effect of raising everything one-half step (A to B♭).

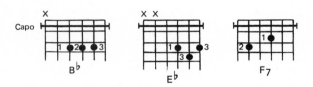

Harmonize and accompany "Oh, Give Thanks."

For $\frac{2}{2}$, use ♩ as the basis for chord selection (two per measure).

Harmonize, play, sing, and accompany "The Muffin Man."

The Muffin Man

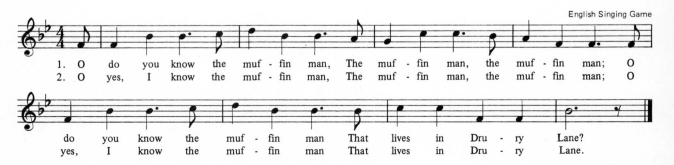

English Singing Game

1. O do you know the muf-fin man, The muf-fin man, the muf-fin man; O do you know the muf-fin man That lives in Dru-ry Lane?
2. O yes, I know the muf-fin man, The muf-fin man, the muf-fin man; O yes, I know the muf-fin man That lives in Dru-ry Lane.

For $\frac{4}{4}$, use ♩ as the basis for chord selection (two per measure).

Play and sing "Now Thank We all Our God."

Now Thank We All Our God

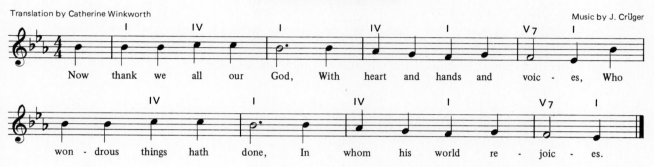

Translation by Catherine Winkworth

Music by J. Crüger

I   IV   I   IV   I   V₇   I

Now thank we all our God, With heart and hands and voic - es, Who

IV   I   IV   I   V₇   I

won - drous things hath done, In whom his world re - joic - es.

The key is E♭ major. B♭, E♭, and A♭ are necessary in the key signature to provide the half and whole step relationships.

1 1 ½ 1 1 1 ½

The primary chords in root position are:

I   IV   V₇

In inversion:

I   IV   V₇

For guitar chords, place a capo on the first fret and use D, G, and A₇ as the primary chords, one fret higher than normally. The capo on the first fret has the effect of raising everything one-half step (D to E♭).

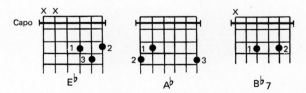

E♭   A♭   B♭₇

Accompany "Now Thank We all Our God," using the harmony indicated.
Harmonize, play, sing and accompany "O Come, Little Children."

O Come, Little Children

Music by J. Schulz

O come, lit-tle chil-dren, O come, one and all. O come to the

cra - dle in Beth - le - hem's stall! And see what the Fa - ther, from

Heav'n high a - bove, Has sent us to - night as a proof of His love.

For $\frac{2}{4}$, use ♩ as the basis for chord selection (one per measure).

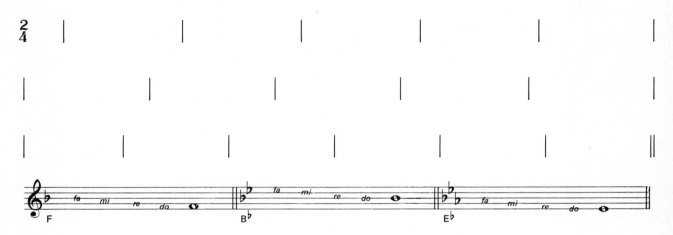

In keys using flats in the signature, the *do* of the major scale is found by calling the last flat *fa* (last on far right), and counting down the interval of a fourth to *do*.

Play each of the following scales on the recorder. Memorize the sequence of flats. It is always the same.

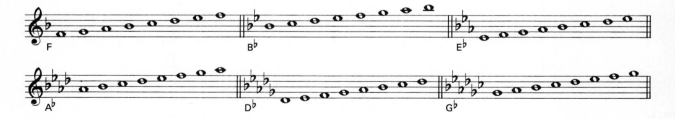

Play these chords on the piano, roots in the left hand and inversions in the right.

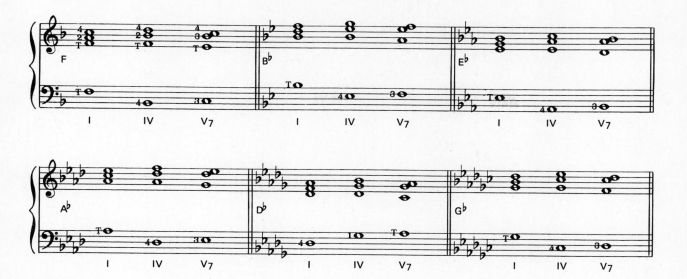

The key of C major plus all sharp and all flat keys form the *circle of fifths*.

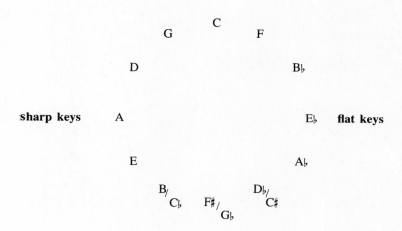

A key counterclockwise is always a fifth higher than its immediate neighbor and has either one less flat *or* one more sharp.

G♭ (6 flats) and F♯ (6 sharps) are *enharmonic* keys, as are B and C♭ (5♯/7♭) and D♭ and C♯ (5♭/7♯).

What is the keynote (*Do*) of each of the following key signatures?

Self-checking Chapter Review

Match Column II to Column I

1. _____ tonic triad (I)
2. _____ subdominant triad (IV)
3. _____ dominant triad (V)
4. _____ dominant seventh (V₇)
5. _____ AB or AABB
6. _____ five-toned scale
7. _____ seven-toned scale
8. _____ 5 whole steps, 2 half steps
9. _____
10. _____
11. _____
12. _____
13. _____
14. _____ SEE ABOVE
15. _____
16. _____ root is lowest sounding
17. _____ root is *not* lowest sounding
18. _____ I, IV, V
19. _____ ii, iii, vi
20. _____ F major chord
21. _____ B♭ major chord
22. _____ C₇ chord
23. _____ device for raising pitch on the guitar

A.   B.   C.   D.

E.

F.

G.

H. heptatonic
I. third
J. *fa-la-do'*
K. binary
L. primary triads
M. capo
N. pentatonic
O. diatonic
P. secondary triads
Q. inversion
R. *sol-ti-re'*
S. root position
T. *sol-ti-re'-fa'*
U. fifth
V. root
W. *do-mi-sol*

Melody *natural minor scale ~ harmonic minor scale ~ melodic minor scale*

Harmony *modulation*

Minor songs have a different sound and feeling from those built on major scales. Play and sing *"Go Down, Moses."*

Go Down, Moses

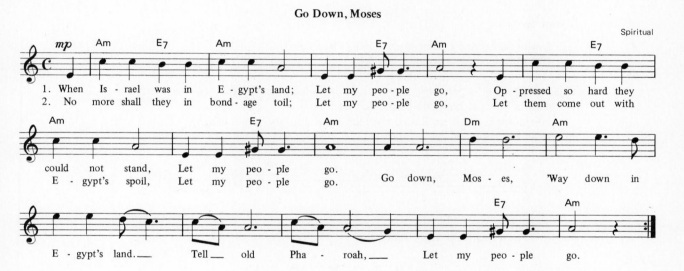

This song is based on a minor scale. Its harmony is minor as well. The notes used, in order, are:

However, since the song clearly centers around an "A," the scale is correctly arranged as:

Note there are no sharps or flats in the key signature but a G♯ consistently appears as an accidental. A minor has the same key signature as C major. For this reason, they are *relative* keys. Each major has a relative minor, and, conversely, every minor has a relative major. Relative keys have the same key signature.

Given the major scale, the relative minor always begins on its *la*.

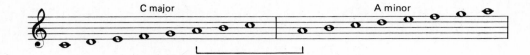

This minor scale begins and ends on *la* with no accidentals. It is called a *natural minor scale.*

Play and sing with syllables the a natural minor scale.

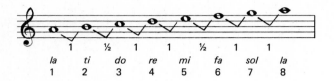

Note there are two half-steps (between *ti-do* and *mi-fa*) as with the major. The scale is thus diatonic. Since the minor begins on *la,* however, these half-steps occur, respectively, between the 2-3 and 5-6 tones.

Listen to

Danse Macabre by Saint–Saens (1835–1921)
(Bowmar Orchestral Library No. 59)

This composition is generally in minor. What is the overall effect? Which instruments are featured? What happens to the tempo?

Harmony is often employed with the natural minor scale, using *la* (1), *re* (4) and *mi* (5) as the roots of the primary triads, respectively. The root positions are:

The inversions are (for right hand):

Each triad, however, is minor—hence, the lower case Roman numerals to designate them.

The natural minor scale is probably the earliest type of minor scale. The harmony is all minor and rarely is a seventh added to v̆. However, as composers continued to use this scale over the years, a chromatic alteration was frequently made. The third of the v̆ triad is raised *one half-step* to provide a major triad as the basis of the chord:

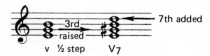

The seventh of the chord is often added, making it a V_7 chord. This change is made to provide a stronger harmony and the chromatic alteration in the scale is known as the *harmonic minor scale.* It differs from the natural minor by only this one tone.

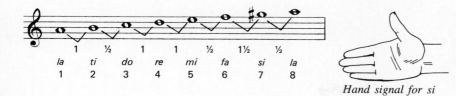

la ti do re mi fa si la
1 2 3 4 5 6 7 8

1 ½ 1 1 ½ 1½ ½

From *SIGHT AND SOUND, TEACHER'S MANUAL* by Arpad Darazs and Stephen Jay. Copyright 1965 by Boosey & Hawkes, Inc. Reprinted by permission.

Hand signal for si

Play and sing the harmonic minor scale with syllables. Compare this scale with the natural minor. *Sol* is used in the natural, *si,* a half step higher, in the harmonic. This chromatic alteration made in the third of the V₇ chord will always be the same. The only tone affected is the 7th tone (*sol-si*) of the scale. Both A natural and A harmonic minor scales are relative to C major because they share the same key signature. The G♯ of A harmonic is only an *accidental* and must be written for *each* measure in which it is intended. It *never* appears as part of the key signature.

Improvise a melody demonstrating the A natural minor scale. Do the same with the A harmonic minor scale.

Accompany "Go Down, Moses" on the guitar and piano. The G♯ accidental in the melody signals the harmonic minor scale, necessitating the E₇ chord.

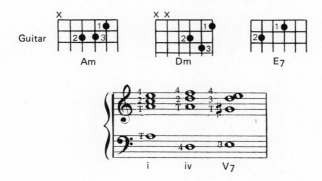

Chording in harmonic minor on piano always follows this pattern.

mi	— ½ step →	fa		mi	— — →	mi
do	whole step →	re		do	whole step →	re
la	— →	la		la	— ½ step →	si
i		iv		i		V₇

Improvise a chord progression in various meters using this formula. Begin and end on i.

Play and sing "March of the Three Kings."

March of the Three Kings

Provençal, 13th Century

One fine day___ I saw a car - a - van ___ of three great kings___ and their roy - al

le - gions,___ One fine day___ I saw a car - a - van ___ of three great

163

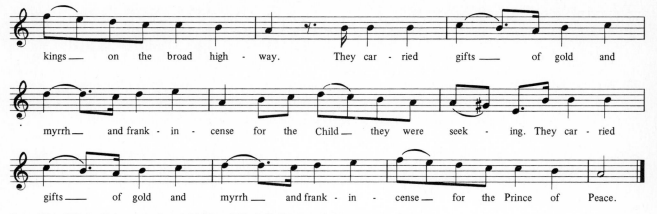

kings __ on the broad high - way. They car - ried gifts __ of gold and myrrh __ and frank - in - cense for the Child __ they were seek - ing. They car - ried gifts __ of gold and myrrh __ and frank - in - cense __ for the Prince of Peace.

From *Music Skills for Classroom Teachers* 4th edition, 1975, Dallin/Winslow (Dubuque: William C. Brown)

Harmony is determined for minor songs just as it is for major, by analyzing melody tones and deciding which chord fits best. Harmonize "March of the Three Kings." The first phrase is harmonized for you. Complete the harmony with i, iv, and V₇ chords and accompany on piano, Autoharp, and guitar.

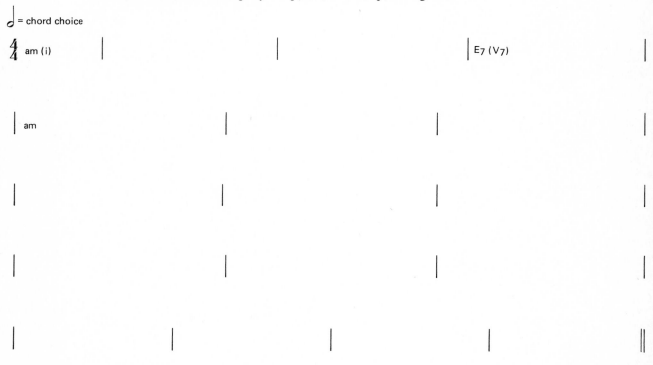

Play and sing "All the Pretty Little Horses."

All the Pretty Little Horses

Southern United States

Hush - a - by, don't you cry, Go to sleep - y, lit - tle ba - by. When you wake you shall have

All the pret - ty lit - tle hor - ses: Blacks and bays, dap - ples and grays, Coach and six - a lit - tle

hor - ses.   Hush - a - by,   don't   you   cry,   Go   to   sleep - y, lit - tle   ba - by.

This is in e minor, relative to G major. Is the song in the natural or harmonic minor?

do   la
                          natural minor

la
                          harmonic minor

The F♯ in the key signature is part of e minor, whether natural or harmonic. Since D♯ is not used as an accidental in the melody, the basis of the song is clearly the natural minor.

Play and sing "Shalom Chaverim." Which type of minor scale is used?

Shalom, Chaverim

Israeli Round

Sha - lom,   cha - ve - rim!   Sha - lom,   cha - ve - rim!   Sha - lom,   sha - lom!   Le -

hit - ra - ot,   le - hit - ra - ot,   sha - lom,   sha - lom.

Accompany "Shalom Chaverim" entirely with an e minor triad and perform as a round. Improvise interesting rhythmic patterns throughout.

It is not always clear in a minor melody which scale is to be used. If the seventh tone (*sol* or *si*) does not appear, harmony can be based on either the natural or harmonic minor. The only difference is between the v̆ and V₇ chord.

Natural

i   iv   v

Bm

Harmonic

i   iv   V(7)

B7

Sing, play, harmonize, and accompany "The Ghost of John." Which scale and chords must be used? Why?

The Ghost of John

Words and Music by Martha Grubb

Have you seen the ghost of John? Long white bones and his skin all gone,

Oo, oo, Would - n't it be chil - ly with no skin on!

For $\frac{4}{4}$, use ♩ as the basis of chord selection (two per measure).

Sing, play, harmonize, and accompany "Winter Holiday." Use either the harmonic or natural minor scale and chords. Why is this possible?

Winter Holiday

Trudi Behar

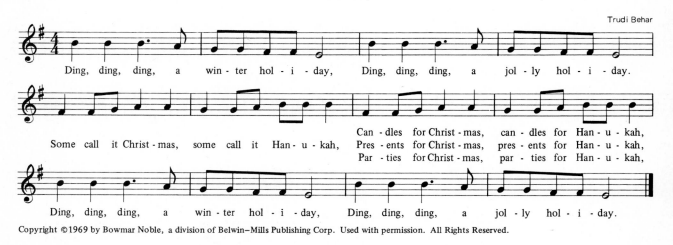

Ding, ding, ding, a win - ter hol - i - day, Ding, ding, ding, a jol - ly hol - i - day.

Some call it Christ - mas, some call it Han - u - kah,
Can - dles for Christ - mas, can - dles for Han - u - kah,
Pres - ents for Christ - mas, pres - ents for Han - u - kah,
Par - ties for Christ - mas, par - ties for Han - u - kah,

Ding, ding, ding, a win - ter hol - i - day, Ding, ding, ding, a jol - ly hol - i - day.

For $\frac{4}{4}$, use ♩ as the basis of chord selection (two per measure).

Play, sing, and accompany "God Rest You Merry, Gentlemen." Harmony has already been provided. It is common for minor songs to *modulate* (change keys) temporarily to the relative major as this one does in the refrain. It ends, however, as it begins, in e minor.

God Rest You Merry, Gentlemen

English Carol

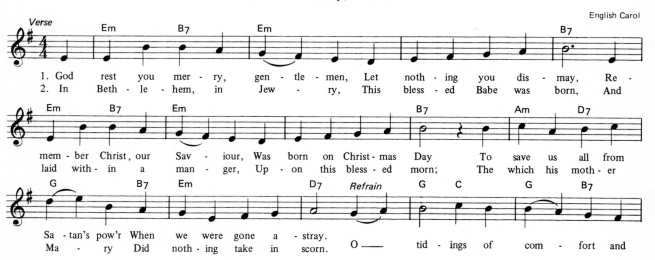

1. God rest you mer - ry, gen - tle - men, Let noth - ing you dis - may, Re -
2. In Beth - le - hem, in Jew - ry, This bless - ed Babe was born, And

mem - ber Christ, our Sav - iour, Was born on Christ - mas Day To save us all from
laid with - in a man - ger, Up - on this bless - ed morn; The which his moth - er

Sa - tan's pow'r When we were gone a - stray.
Ma - ry Did noth - ing take in scorn. O tid - ings of com - fort and

joy, com-fort and joy, O —— tid - ings of com - fort and joy.

Play and Sing "On Halloween." What is the key? Natural or harmonic? What is the relative major?

On Halloween

Mysteriously

Max T. Krone

1. Gob - lins, al - ley cats, witch - es on brooms, Wind in the trees sing - ing scar - y tunes,
2. Rat - tling skel - e - tons, spooks in white, Moan - ing and groan - ing,— through the night,

These are the things that are heard and seen, In the dark of night, on Ha - low - een.

d minor is relative to F major. Since C is not used in the melody, it is not clear whether the natural or harmonic minor is intended. Harmony could be provided with either.

do ——→ la

i iv v i iv V₇

Harmonize and accompany "On Halloween."

For $\frac{4}{4}$, use ♩ as the basis for chord selection (two per measure).

Improvise additional ostinatos.

Play, sing, harmonize, and accompany each of the following: Be certain to de-cide which minor scale is intended. If you have a choice, you may use either.

Black   cats!   Hal - low - een.   Witch - es   on   Broom - sticks.

Candles of Hanukah

Adapted by Roberta McLaughlin
and Lucille Wood

1. Burn, lit - tle can - dles, burn, burn, burn, Han - u - kah is here.
2. Eight lit - tle can - dles, in a row, Han - u - kah is here.
3. Dance, lit - tle can - dles, dance, dance, dance, Han - u - kah is here.

Burn, lit - tle can - dles, burn, burn, burn, Burn - ing bright and clear.
Eight lit - tle can - dles, in a row, Burn - ing bright and clear.
Dance, lit - tle can - dles, dance, dance, dance, Burn - ing bright and clear.

Copyright ©1969 by Bowmar Noble, a division of Belwin–Mills Publishing Corp. Used with permission. All Rights Reserved.

For $\frac{4}{4}$, use ○ as the basis for chord selection (one per measure).

The Tailor and the Mouse

English Folk Song

Verse

1. There was a tai - lor had a mouse;   They lived to - geth - er
2. The tai - lor tho't the mouse was ill; Hi - did - dle un - kum fee - dle! Be - cause he took an
3. And so he gave him cat - nip tea;   Un - til a heart - y

Refrain

in one house; Hi - did - dle - un - kum fee - dle!   Hi - did - dle un - kum tar - um, tan - tum!
a - gue chill; Hi - did - dle un - kum fee - dle!
mouse was he;

Thro' the town of Ram - say; Hi - did - dle un - kum, o - ver the lea, Hi - did - dle un - kum fee - dle!

For $\frac{4}{4}$, use ○ as the basis for chord selection (one per measure).

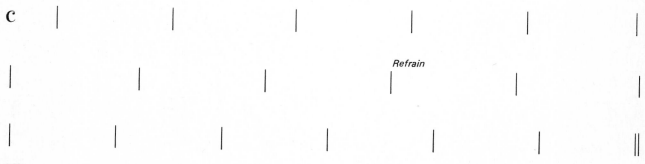

Refrain

168

For $\frac{4}{4}$, use ○ as the basis for chord selection (one per measure).
Play and sing "Lully, Lullay."

Lully, Lullay
(Coventry Carol)

Traditional English Carol

Lul - ly, lul - lay, thou lit - tle ti - ny child, By, by, lul - ly, lul - lay. _____ Lul -

lay, thou lit - tle ti - ny child, By, by, lul - ly, lul - lay. _____

What is the key? Which type of minor scale is indicated? What is the relative major?

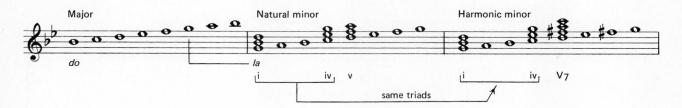

Harmonize and accompany "Lully, Lullay."

For $\frac{3}{4}$, use ♩. as the basis for chord selection (one per measure).

Improvise rhythmic accompaniments which are appropriate.
Sing, play, harmonize, and accompany each of the following:

Poor Mister Wind

Lucille Wood

Sadly

1. Poor Mis - ter Wind! Poor Mis - ter Wind! Has lost his hap - py song, _____ Has
2. Poor Mis - ter Wind! Poor Mis - ter Wind! He lost it in the tree - tops, He
3. Poor Mis - ter Wind! Poor Mis - ter Wind! The rain is cry - ing soft - ly, The

lost his hap - py song. _____ Poor Mis - ter Wind! Poor Mis - ter Wind!
lost it in the tree - tops. Poor Mis - ter Wind! Poor Mis - ter Wind!
rain is cry - ing soft - ly. Poor Mis - ter Wind! Poor Mis - ter Wind!

For $\frac{4}{4}$, use 𝅝 as the basis for chord selection (one per measure.)

Eight Nights of Hanukah

Words by Freda Prensky

Hebrew Folk Tune

Flick - er, lit - tle can - dles, flick - er bright for Ha - nu - kah, Flick - er, lit - tle can - dles,

all eight nights of Ha - nu - kah. Lit - tle tops are spin - ning

round and round on Ha - nu - kah, Lit - tle tops are spin - ning, Ha - nu - kah is here.

Used by permission of Judith K. Eisenstein. From SONGS OF CHILDHOOD.

For $\frac{4}{4}$, use 𝅗𝅥 as the basis for chord selection (four per measure).

Since every major key has a relative minor, the circle of fifths may be written to show these as well.

$$C/a$$
$$G/e \qquad F/d$$
$$D/b \qquad B\flat/g$$
$$A/f\sharp \qquad E\flat/c$$
$$E/c\sharp \qquad A\flat/f$$
$$B/g\sharp \qquad D\flat/b\flat$$
$$C\flat/a\flat \quad F\sharp/d\sharp \quad C\sharp/a\sharp$$
$$G\flat/e\flat$$

Remember: The minor scale has the same key signature as the major but begins and ends on *la*. The *natural* minor has no chromatic alterations but the *harmonic* minor has a raised seventh step, that is, *sol* becomes *si*. This *always* appears as an accidental but *never* in the key signature.

Complete the following scales:

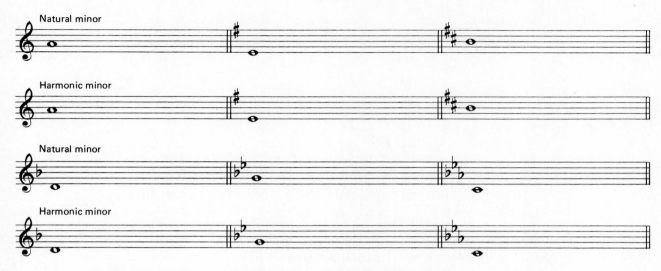

Sing, play, harmonize, and accompany "Dreydl Spin."

Dreydl Spin

Translated by Eugene W. Troth

Israeli Folk Song

Moderato, accented

Drey - dl spin, drey - dl spin, Ha - nu - kah is a day of joy; Drey - dl spin, drey - dl spin,

Ha - nu - kah is a day of joy; Oh, how great the an - cient mir - a - cle, drey - dl spin, Oh,

drey - dl spin, Oh, how great the an - cient mir - a - cle, drey - dl spin, oh drey - dl spin.

Reprinted by permission of D.C. Heath and Company.

For $\frac{2}{4}$, use ♩ as the basis for chord selection (two per measure).

$\frac{2}{4}$

A third species of the minor scale, less frequently used, is one in which there are chromatic alterations of the sixth and seventh tones when the melody is ascending.

fa   si   la   sol   fa

Fa is raised to *fi, sol* to *si* ascending, but returned to *fa* and *sol* descending.

Hand signal for fi

From SIGHT AND SOUND, TEACHER'S MANUAL by Arpad Darazs and Stephen Jay. Copyright 1965 by Boosey & Hawkes, Inc. Reprinted by permission.

The descending version is identical to the natural minor in that the sixth and seventh tones are returned to their normal pitches. This species is called the *melodic minor* scale. Its use does not produce new harmony, however, since either the v̌ or V₇ may be used, depending on the chromatic alteration at that point. These alterations appear always as accidentals. (A raised natural becomes ♯ a raised flat becomes ♮.)

Complete the melodic minor scale (ascending and descending) for each of the following:

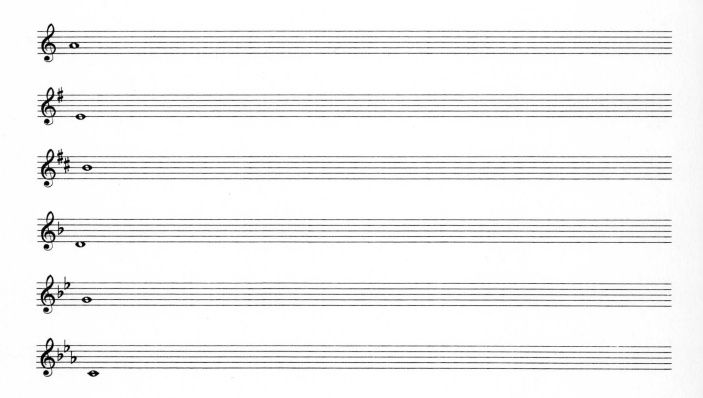

Self-checking Chapter Review

Match these major keys with their relative minors in Column II . . .

1. _____ C	A. e
2. _____ B	B. b
3. _____ A	C. f♯
4. _____ F	D. b♭
5. _____ G	E. d♯
6. _____ F♯	F. g♯
7. _____ E♭	G. f
8. _____ D♭	H. c
9. _____ D	I. d
10. _____ A♭	J. e♭
11. _____ B♭	K. a
12. _____ E	L. c♯
13. _____ G♭	M. g

. . . and these chords with their correct fingerings.

14. _____ b minor chord	N.
15. _____ B₇ chord	O.
16. _____ a minor chord	P.
17. _____ d minor chord	Q.
18. _____ E₇ chord	R.

What *one* note is needed to change each of the following to the harmonic minor scale?

19   20   21

22   23   24

What *two* notes are needed to change each of the above scales to the *ascending* melodic minor scale?

25. _____
26. _____
27. _____
28. _____
29. _____
30. _____

Melody   *range*
Harmony   *transposition*

A variety of keys, both major and minor, exist with which composers can write music. Knowing a variety of keys enables a practical musician to move a song from one key to another. *Transposition* is changing a song from one key, say E♭ major, to another key, such as C major. *Transposing* means pitching the melody as well as interpreting the harmony in the new key. The only element not affected by transposition is the rhythm.

Sing and play "Drink to Me Only With Thine Eyes" in the original key of E♭ major and then in the transposed version in C major.

Drink to Me Only With Thine Eyes

Old English Air
Ben Johnson (1573?–1637)

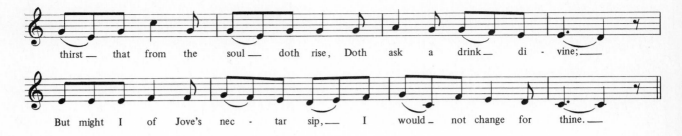

thirst — that from the soul — doth rise, Doth ask a drink — di - vine;

But might I of Jove's nec - tar sip, — I would — not change for thine. —

Why is transposition necessary? Sometimes the *range* of a piece, its lowest to highest pitches, is too high (or low) for a group to sing. Transposition will place the range of a song within the range of the singers. Also, some keys are difficult to perceive and work with, such as F♯ major (six sharps) on the piano. Transposing the song down one half step to F major (one flat) may enable the person at the keyboard to function more easily. This can be true for guitar chords as well. It is easier to play in D major on the guitar than in E♭ major (without the capo, at least), and an accompaniment might be transposed down because the chords are easier to play.

Many musicians learn to transpose by ear once the melody and chord progressions have been learned. Beginners find it necessary to first write out the melody and harmony.

Listen to

"March to the Scaffold" from *Symphonie Fantastique* by Berlioz (1803–1869) (Bowmar Orchestral Library No. 78)

The following melody is heard in several transposed versions throughout the movement.

Allegretto non troppo

"MARCH TO THE SCAFFOLD" from The Bowmar Orchestral Library "Musical Kaleidoscope" (No. 093) by Lucille Wood Copyright © 1967 by Bowmar Noble, a division of Belwin–Mills Publishing Corp. Used With Permission. All Rights Reserved.

What is the contour of the melody? What instruments play it? What is the overall effect of the piece? Why?

Play and sing "Marching to Pretoria."

Marching to Pretoria

English translation by Josef Marais

South Africa

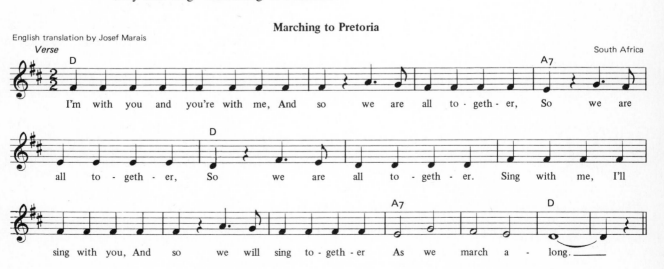

I'm with you and you're with me, And so we are all to - geth - er, So we are

all to - geth - er, So we are all to - geth - er. Sing with me, I'll

sing with you, And so we will sing to - geth - er As we march a - long. ___

176

We are march-ing to Pre - to - ri - a,_____ Pre - to - ri - a,

— Pre - to - ri - a,_____ We are march-ing to Pre -

to - ri - a,_____ Pre - to - ri - a, hur - rah!_____

The steps for transposing a song are:
1. Determine the key, scale and chords of the song:

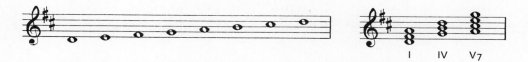

I   IV   V₇

2. Using syllables, assign each pitch in the scale its respective name. (Include chords, too.)

do   re   mi   fa   sol   la   ti   do

3. Determine the respective syllable of each pitch in the song according to the designations above.

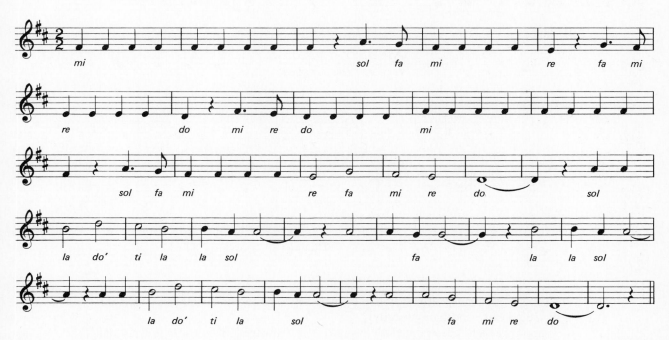

mi   sol   fa   mi   re   fa   mi

re   do   mi   re   do   mi

sol   fa   mi   re   fa   mi   re   do   sol

la   do'   ti   la   la   sol   fa   la   la   sol

la   do'   ti   la   sol   fa   mi   re   do

4. Write the scale of the key to which the song is to be transposed and assign each tone in this scale its respective syllable name.

do   re   mi   fa   sol   la   ti   do'   I   IV   V7

5. Rewrite the pitches by interpreting the syllables (formula) of the song in the new key, maintaining the melodic contour of the original.

6. Add the rhythms and chord symbols and interpret in the new key.

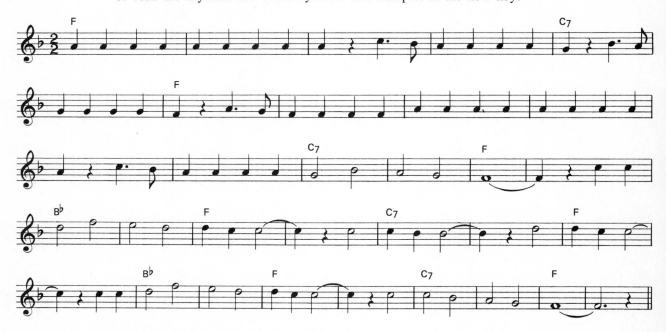

The song is now transposed. Play it in the new key to be certain it sounds as it should, both melodically and harmonically.

Improvise a three–tone melody using G A B. Transpose it by ear to A B C♯ and D E F♯.

178

Sing "Pop Goes the Weasel."

Pop Goes the Weasel

American Square Dance Tune

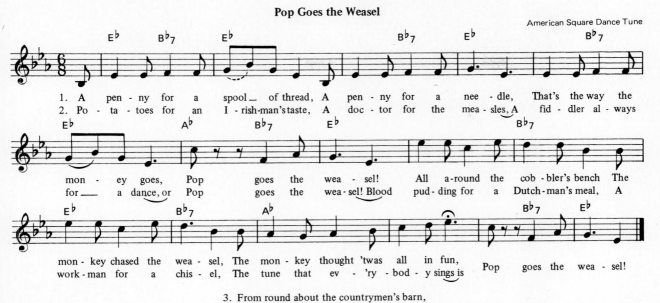

1. A pen - ny for a spool __ of thread, A pen - ny for a nee - dle, That's the way the
2. Po - ta - toes for an I - rish-man's taste, A doc - tor for the mea - sles, A fid - dler al - ways

mon - ey goes, Pop goes the wea - sel! All a-round the cob - bler's bench The
for __ a dance, or Pop goes the wea - sel! Blood pud - ding for a Dutch-man's meal, A

mon - key chased the wea - sel, The mon - key thought 'twas all in fun, Pop goes the wea - sel!
work - man for a chis - el, The tune that ev - 'ry - bod - y sings is Pop goes the wea - sel!

3. From round about the countrymen's barn,
   The mice begin to mizzle;
   For when they poke their noses out,
   Pop goes the weasel!
   The painter works with ladder and brush,
   The artist with the easel,
   The fiddler always snaps the strings at
   Pop goes the weasel!

Transpose "Pop Goes the Weasel" to F major so it can be played on the recorder.
Complete the following steps.

1. Determine the key and scale and chords of the song:

2. Assign each pitch its respective syllable name.

sol do re mi fa sol la ti do'

3. Interpret each pitch of the song by syllables, as shown in the first line.

sol do do re re mi sol mi do sol

179

4. Write the scale and syllables of the key to which the song is to be transposed.

do re mi fa sol la ti do' sol   I   IV   V7

5. Interpret in the new key the syllables in #3 above, maintaining the melodic contour of the original. Complete the following:

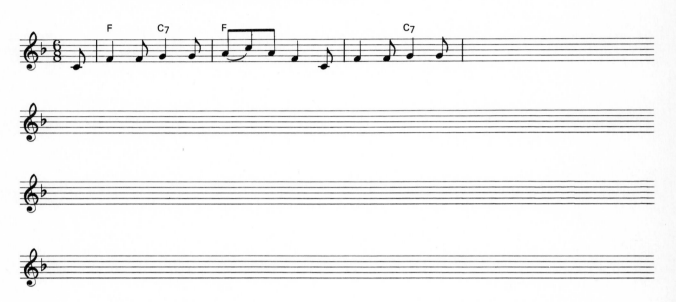

6. Add the rhythms and chord symbols, interpreting in the new key.

Play the transposed version of "*Pop Goes the Weasel.*" Check the harmony too.
Play and sing "Who Did?"

Who Did?

American Folk Song

1. Who did, who did, who did, who did, Who did swal - low Jo - Jo - Jo - nah?
2. Whale did, whale did, whale did, whale did, Whale did swal - low Jo - Jo - Jo - nah.

Who did, who did, who did, who did, Who did swal - low Jo - Jo - Jo - nah?
Whale did, whale did, whale did, whale did, Whale did swal - low Jo - Jo - Jo - nah.

Who did, who did, who did, who did, Who did, swal - low Jo - Jo - Jo - nah?
Whale did, whale did, whale did, whale did, Whale did swal - low Jo - Jo - Jo - nah.

Who did swal-low Jo - nah? Who did swal-low Jo - nah? Who did swal-low Jo - nah down?
Whale did, swal-low Jo - nah. Whale did swal-low Jo - nah. Whale did swal-low Jo - nah down.

Transpose to the key of A major (three sharps) by following the given outline.

1.

I IV V₇

2.

sol la ti do re mi fa sol la ti do'

3. Place syllables under the notes of the actual song above.

4.

sol la ti do re mi fa sol la ti do' I IV V₇

5. and 6. Combine on the same staff.

Play your transposed version. Check the harmony too.
Play and sing "Sing Your Way Home."

Sing Your Way Home

Traditional Camper's Song

Smoothly

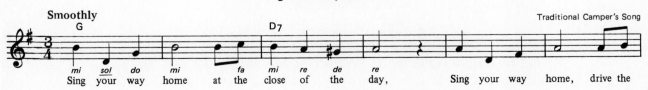

mi sol do mi fa mi re de re
Sing your way home at the close of the day, Sing your way home, drive the

181

shad - ows a - way. Smile ev - 'ry mile, for wher - ev - er you roam It will

bright - en your road, It will light - en your load, If you sing your way home.

Transpose to F major by following the same six steps.

1.

2.
raised   raised
do = de re = ri

3. Place syllables under notes of the actual song above.

4.
de   ri

5. and 6.

Play your transposed version. Check the harmony too.

There are some easy transpositions which involve changing a key signature only:

From D♭ major to D major

From D♭ major to D major

Change the key signature from five flats to two sharps and read the pitches accordingly.

182

From E major to E♭ major

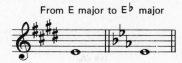

From E major to E♭ major

Change the key signature from four sharps to three flats.
From F♯ major to F major

From F♯ major to F major

Change the key signature from six sharps to one flat.
What other easy transpositions can you think of from A♭ major and B major?
A♭ major (four flats)

A♭ major (four flats)

B major (five sharps)

B major (five sharps)

Transpositions in minor are handled with the same six steps outlined above.
Play and sing "Old House."

Old House

American Folk Game Song
Collected by John W. Work

Solo — Old   house.   Chorus — Tear it down!   Solo — Who's going to help me?   Chorus — Tear it down!
la   do.   la   do.   mi   do   la

Solo — Bring me a ham-mer.   Chorus — Tear it down!   Solo — Bring me a saw. —   Chorus — Tear it down!

Solo — Next thing you bring me,   Chorus — Tear it down!   Solo — Is a wreck-ing ma-chine.   Chorus — Tear it down!

2. New house. Build it up!
   Who's going to help me? Build it up!
   Bring me a hammer. Build it up!
   Bring me a saw. Build it up!
   Next thing you bring me, Build it up!
   Is a carpenter man. Build it up!

Transpose to d minor.

1. Determine the key, scale and chords of the original song.

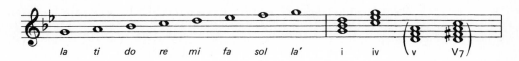

la ti do re mi fa sol la'   i   iv   (v   V₇)

(Can't really tell whether it is natural or harmonic.)

2. Assign syllables.
3. Place syllables in the song. (See song above.)
4. Write the new scale with syllables.

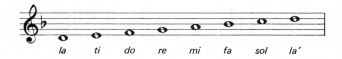

la   ti   do   re   mi   fa   sol   la'

5. and 6. Rewrite pitches in the new key. Add the rhythms and chord symbols for the new key.

Play the transposed version of "Old House."

Play and sing "Bird's Courting Song."

Bird's Courting Song

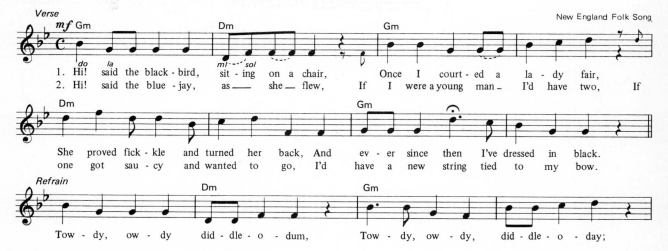

New England Folk Song

1. Hi! said the black-bird, sit-ing on a chair, Once I court-ed a la-dy fair,
2. Hi! said the blue-jay, as she flew, If I were a young man I'd have two, If

She proved fick-kle and turned her back, And ev-er since then I've dressed in black.
one got sau-cy and wanted to go, I'd have a new string tied to my bow.

Refrain

Tow-dy, ow-dy did-dle-o-dum, Tow-dy, ow-dy, did-dle-o-day;

Tow - dy, ow - dy did - dle - o - dum, Tow - dy, ow - dy, did - dle - o - day.

3. "Hi!" said the little leather-winged bat,
   "I will tell you the reason that,
   The reason that I fly in the night,
   Is because I've lost my heart's delight."

4. "Hi!" said the swallow, sitting on a barn,
   "Courting, I think, it is no harm,
   I pick my feathers and sit up straight,
   And hope ev'ry young man will pick his mate."

From *Growing With Music,* Wilson et al, Book 5. (Englewood Cliffs, NJ: Prentice–Hall, Inc., 1966)

Transpose to a minor, following the same six steps.

1.

2.

3. Use song above.

4.

5. and 6.

Play your transposed version. Check the harmony too.

Sometimes a minor song is transposed to major or vice versa. Composers use this as a means to provide variety. The simplest way is to transpose by parallel keys (scales that have the same keynote), such as C major and c minor, or G major and g minor. Here is an example:

One fine day,___ I saw a car - a - van ___ of three great kings and their roy - al

Transposing from minor to major and vice versa means changing key signatures and interpreting the pitches accordingly. The chords are still the primary ones, but interpreted in the new key.

To change C major to c minor, add three flats.
To change a minor to A major, add three sharps.
To change D major to d minor, drop two sharps and add one flat.

How would you—

change Eb major to eb minor?
f minor to F major?
g minor to G major?
E major to e minor?

Transpose "Halloween Sounds" to its parallel minor.

Halloween Sounds

Lucille Wood

1. This is the way____ the witch - es fly, witch - es fly, witch - es fly,
2. This is the way____ the ghosts go by, ghosts go by, ghosts go by,

This is the way____ the witch - es fly, Swish, Swish, Swish.
This is the way____ the ghosts go by, Oh! Oh! Oh!

3. This is the way the tomcats howl, tomcats howl, tomcats howl.
   This is the way the tomcats howl, Meow! Meow! Meow!
4. This is the way the pumpkins laugh, pumpkins laugh, pumpkins laugh.
   This is the way the pumpkins laugh, Hee! Hee! Hee!
5. This is the way the hoot owls cry, hoot owls cry, hoot owls cry.
   This is the way the hoot owls cry, Hoo, hoo, hoo.

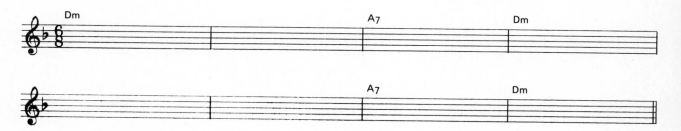

Play both versions.

In transposition, no matter what major key, the following formula applies to the keyboard:

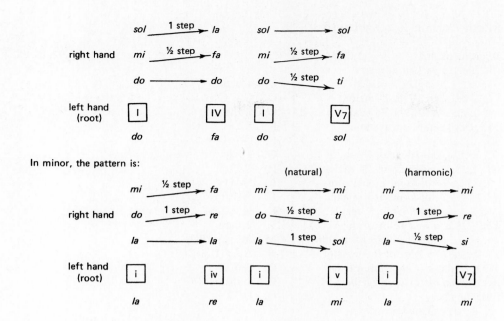

In minor, the pattern is:

Improvise a short recorder or piano melody using D E F G A. Transpose it by ear to G A B♭ C D.

As mentioned earlier, the capo is used on the guitar to transpose chords to higher keys. The net effect of using the capo is to raise any given chord one-half step for each fret the capo covers.

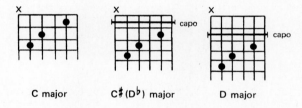

C major   C♯(D♭) major   D major

This allows an instant type of transposition.

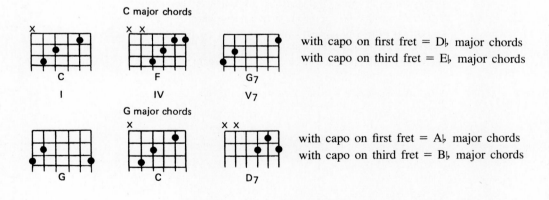

with capo on first fret = D♭ major chords
with capo on third fret = E♭ major chords

with capo on first fret = A♭ major chords
with capo on third fret = B♭ major chords

The capo is not generally affective beyond the third fret because the strings lose much of their resonance.

What is the effect of using A major chords (A, D, E₇) with the capo on the first fret? on the second fret?

What is the effect of using D major chords (D,G,A₇) with the capo on the first fret? on the second fret? on the third fret?

What other instant transpositions can you figure out using the capo?

Match Column II to Column I.

What tones are:

1. _____ in I in C major
2. _____ in I in A major
3. _____ in IV in D major
4. _____ in IV in B♭ major
5. _____ in V₇ in F major
6. _____ in V₇ in G major
7. _____ *mi-re-do* in C major
8. _____ *mi-re-do* in E♭ major
9. _____ *sol-la-mi* in G major
10. _____ *sol-la-mi* in F major
11. _____ *fa-mi-re* in D major
12. _____ *fa-mi-re* in B♭ major
13. _____ *do'-la-sol* in E♭ major
14. _____ *do'-la-sol* in A major

What is the key signature of the *parallel minor* of each of the following?

15. _____ G major
16. _____ A major
17. _____ D major
18. _____ F major

What is the key signature of the *parallel major* of each of the following?

19. _____ g minor
20. _____ e♭ minor
21. _____ e minor
22. _____ b minor

A. E♭ C B♭
B. 4 flats
C. C E G B♭
D. 1 sharp
E. E D C
F. D E B
G. 3 flats
H. C E G
I. E♭ D C
J. 5 sharps
K. E♭ G B♭
L. 2 flats
M. 0 sharps/flats
N. A C♯ E
O. G F E♭
P. 4 sharps
Q. D F♯ A C
R. G F♯ E
S. 1 flat
T. A F♯ E
U. C D A
V. G B D

188

14

Melody	passing tones ~ modes ~ whole-tone scale
Rhythm	asymmetric meter ~ changing meter ~ polyrhythm
Harmony	modulation ~ secondary dominant ~ supertonic

Play, sing and accompany "When Johnny Comes Marching Home."

When Johnny Comes Marching Home

Words and Music by Louis Lambert

1. When John-ny comes march-ing home a-gain, Hur-rah,___ Hur-rah!___ We'll give him a heart-y wel-come then, Hur-rah,___ Hur-rah!___ The___ men will cheer,___ the boys will shout, The la - dies, they___ will all turn out, And we'll all feel gay, when John-ny comes march-ing home! ___

2. The old___ church bell will peal a-gain, Hur-rah,___ Hur-rah!___ To wel-come home our dar-ling boy, Hur-rah,___ Hur-rah!___ The___ vil-lage lads___ and las-sies gay, With ros - es they___ will strew the way,

3. Get ready for the Jubilee, Hurrah, Hurrah!
We'll give the hero three times three, Hurrah, Hurrah!
The laurel wreath is ready now To place upon his loyal brow,
And we'll all feel gay, when Johnny comes marching home!

The song begins and ends in g minor. There is a brief departure to the relative major, particularly in the third line. A change of tonality within a composition is called *modulation*. Short folk songs seldom modulate but longer compositions frequently do to provide variety. A symphony listed in G major, for example, may only begin and end in G major. In between, it may modulate to many keys. A very common modulation is between relative majors and minors. "When Johnny Comes Marching Home" modulates from g minor to B♭ major and back to g minor; there is no change of key signature.

minor   major

189

Listen to

American Salute by Gould (1913–   )
(Bowmar Orchestral Library No. 65)

"When Johnny Comes Marching Home" is used as a theme for a set of variations. Is modulation a means whereby the composer provides variation? How else is variety provided? What provides the unity?

An effect close to modulation may occur when *secondary* dominants are used. A secondary dominant is a chromatically altered chord which establishes a note (and chord) other than the tonic as a temporary tonal center.

Play, sing, and accompany "I'm a Yankee Doodle Dandy."

I'm a Yankee Doodle Dandy

Words and Music by George M. Cohan

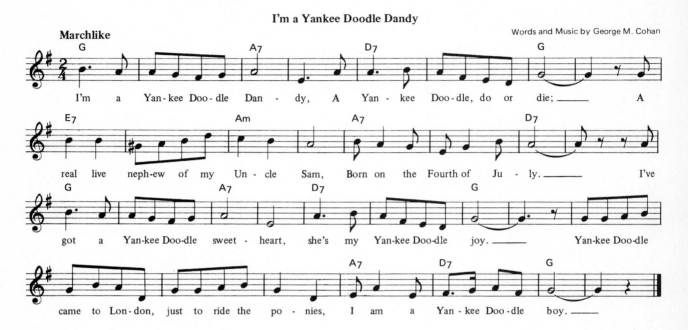

The primary chords in this key are:

I   IV   V₇

However, A_7 and E_7 both occur. These chords are used to establish temporarily D and A, respectively, as a tonic (tonal center).

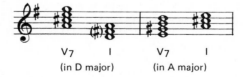

V₇   I   V₇   I
(in D major)   (in A major)

A_7 in G major may be considered the dominant of D_7 (the V_7 of V_7). E_7 in G major may be considered the dominant of A (the V_7 of the 2nd scale degree, ii, the *supertonic*).

Secondary dominants may be signaled by accidentals in the melody. Since their tones will probably be outside the original key signatures, accidentals may be needed.

Play, sing, and accompany "*Give My Regards to Broadway*." What two chords appear as secondary dominants?

190

Give My Regards to Broadway

Words and Music by George M. Cohan

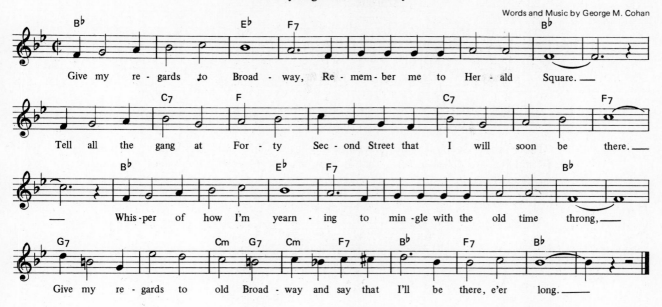

Give my re - gards to Broad - way, Re - mem - ber me to Her - ald Square. — Tell all the gang at For - ty Sec - ond Street that I will soon be there. — — Whis - per of how I'm yearn - ing to min - gle with the old time throng, — Give my re - gards to old Broad - way and say that I'll be there, e'er long. —

Play, sing, and accompany "Meet Me in St. Louis, Louis." What three chords appear as secondary dominants?

Meet Me In St Louis, Louis

Words by Andrew Sterling

Music by Kerry Mills

Waltzlike

Meet me in St. Lou - is, Lou - is, Meet me at the fair; — Don't tell me the lights are shin - ing an - y place but there. — We will dance the Hooch - ee Kooch - ee, — I will be your toot - sie woot - sie; — Meet me in St. Lou - is, Lou - is, Meet me at the fair. —

Not every accidental signals a secondary dominant, however. Some are only decorative *non-harmonic tones*. Play, sing, and accompany "Hawaiian Rainbows."

Hawaiian Rainbows

Hawaiian Folk Song

Ha - wai - ian rain - bows, white clouds roll by; You show your

col - ors   a - gainst the   sky.   Ha - wai - ian   rain - bows,   it   seems   to

me,   Reach   from   the   moun - tain   down   to   the   sea.

There are no secondary dominants in this song. Chromatic accidentals, such as the F♮ and B♭, are *passing tones,* that is, they are non-harmonic tones that pass between chord tones.

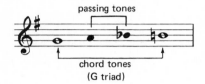

Where are other such examples in this song?

Play, sing and, accompany "Changing of the Guard." Where is there a brief modulation? Where are there passing tones?

Changing of the Guard

Words by George K. Evans

Music by Georges Bizet

1. Here we come to   change the guard,   March - ing down the   bou - le - vard,   Blow trum pets,
2. Sa - bers rat - tling   by   our side,   Ev - 'ry sol - dier   keeps in stride,   *Son - ne, trom -*
3. *A - vec la gar - de   mon - tante,   Nous ar - ri - vons, nous voi - là!*

beat on the drum,   Ra - ta - ta - ta - ta - ta - tum!   Like tin sol diers,   full   of   pep,
pette é cla - tante,   Ra - ta - ta - ta - ta - ta - ta!   Here we come to   change the guard,
                                                              Nous mar - chons la   tê - te haute,

Eyes a - head, and   all   in step,   Blow trum - pets,   beat on the drum,   Ra - ta - ta - ta - tum!
Mov - ing down the   bou - le - vard,
Com - me de pe - tits sol - dats,   *Mar quant sans   fai - re de faute,   Ra - ta - ta - ta - ta!*

From *Growing With Music,* Wilson, et al, Book 5 (Englewood Cliffs, NJ: (Prentice-Hall, Inc., 1966)

Major, minor, and pentatonic scales are the most common. The chromatic scale is rarely used in folk music. There are several scales that were used in medieval times and which have been rediscovered by contemporary composers. These are called the *modes.*

Play and sing "Sabbath Evening."

Sabbath Evening

Judith K. Eisenstein
(From an Old Synagogue Chant)

Now the Sab - bath An - gel May look in - to our win - dow, For Moth - er's light - ing can - dles And ev - 'ry - one's at home. Sha - bat ____ Sha - lom.

Used by permission of Judith K. Eisenstein. From *Gateway To Jewish Songs*.

Although the key signature seems to indicate E♭ major, a D♭ consistently appears in the song as an accidental, making the scale:

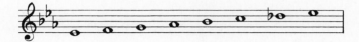

This is called the *mixolydian mode*. It is very similar to a major scale except that it has a lowered seventh step.

Improvise a short melody using E♭ mixolydian.

Here is the mixolydian in C. Play and sing it.

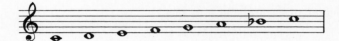

Here is the mixolydian in F. Play and sing it.

Write the mixolydian scale in G, D, B♭ and A. Play the results.

Other modes include the *dorian*, which is like a major scale with a lowered third and seventh degree,

the *phrygian*, which is like major with a lowered second, third, sixth and seventh degree,

and the *lydian*, which is like major with a raised 4th degree.

What is the half-whole step arrangements of each of these modes:
    dorian?
    phrygian?
    lydian?
    mixolydian?
Improvise melodies in each of these modes.

Identify each of the following modes by name (i.e. C lydian, etc.). Play each.

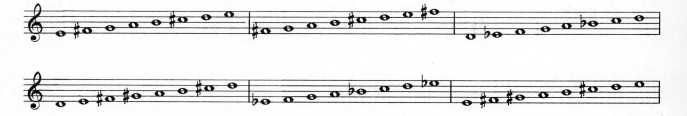

Write the following modes on the given keynote. Play each.

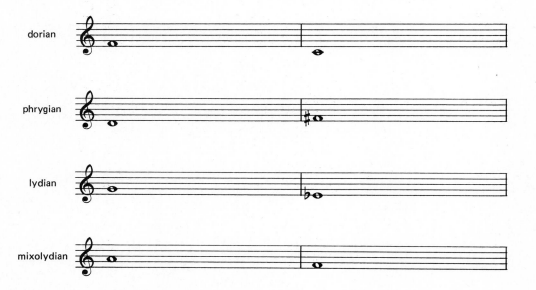

194

Find a song in C major and change it to one of the modes by adding accidentals. Play and sing the results.

Modes were gradually superseded by the major and minor tonalities in the 17th and 18th centuries. Twentieth century composers in all categories—symphonic, folk, pop, and jazz—have turned to these as a new source of melodic and harmonic material.

Another scale that has been used in the twentieth century is the *whole-tone scale,* consisting entirely of whole steps. Play and sing this whole-tone scale.

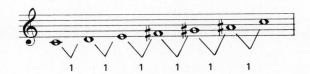

Play "When the Saints . . ." written in the whole-tone scale.

Improvise a melody in the whole-tone scale. In addition to a variety of scales, music of this century has used asymmetrical meters, those that are not duple, triple or quadruple. "Gerakina" is in $\frac{7}{8}$ but subdivided into SwwSwSw or $\frac{3}{8} + \frac{2}{8} + \frac{2}{8}$. (♩♪♪♩♩) Clap the melodic rhythm. Play and sing.

Gerakina

English Words by Margaret Marks

Greek Folk Song

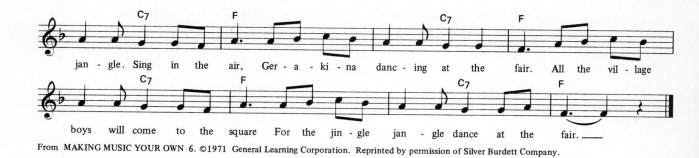

jan - gle. Sing in the air, Ger - a - ki - na danc - ing at the fair. All the vil - lage

boys will come to the square For the jin - gle jan - gle dance at the fair. ___

From MAKING MUSIC YOUR OWN 6. ©1971 General Learning Corporation. Reprinted by permission of Silver Burdett Company.

Create rhythms for these meters.

Write a song (8 measures) using an asymmetrical meter with the whole-tone scale.

Improvise a rhythmic accompaniment in the same meter.

Changing meter is when the metric grouping changes often, possibly in each measure. Clap the following:

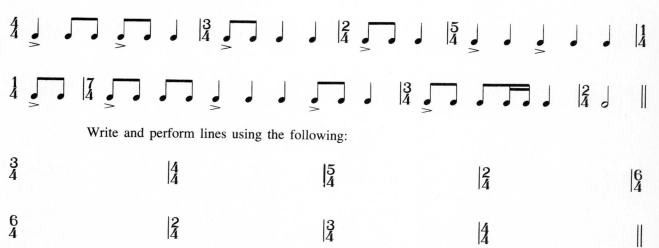

Write and perform lines using the following:

$\frac{3}{4}$ $\left|\frac{4}{4}\right.$ $\left|\frac{5}{4}\right.$ $\left|\frac{2}{4}\right.$ $\left|\frac{6}{4}\right.$

$\frac{6}{4}$ $\left|\frac{2}{4}\right.$ $\left|\frac{3}{4}\right.$ $\left|\frac{4}{4}\right.$ $\|$

Write a composition using one of the modes with the changing meters you wrote above. Add words. Play and sing.

Polyrhythms occur when two or more parts, performed simultaneously, have accents (strong beats) which do not coincide. This occurs in much twentieth century music.

Clap each of the following separately:

Now perform as a trio simultaneously.

Repeat with a separate rhythm instrument on each line.

Write a twenty-four beat composition in three parts to demonstrate polyrhythms. Add instruments and perform.

$(\quad = \quad . = \quad)$
Part I $\frac{4}{4}$
Part II $\frac{9}{8}$
Part III $\frac{6}{4}$

Practice each of these lines. Play on classroom percussion. Play on select recorder tones or guitar/Autoharp/piano chords where appropriate.

Play "Are You Sleeping" as written.

Practice this pattern on the piano.

L.H.   R.H.

Sing and play the melody as written while you accompany with the $\frac{3}{4}$ piano ostinato. (You will play it eleven times.)

This is another example of polyrhythms. Create another example with a well known song. Improvise rhythmic accompaniments.

Match the following notation with the terms listed below.

(in C major)

I chord

H. ii

I. | notation |

J. | notation |

1. _____ secondary dominant
2. _____ passing tones
3. _____ asymmetrical meter
4. _____ dorian mode
5. _____ changing meter
6. _____ lydian mode
7. _____ whole-tone scale
8. _____ mixolydian mode
9. _____ supertonic
10. _____ phrygian mode

Glossary

absolute music   abstract music which is not based on a story or picture; pure music without extra-musical references.

accelerando   to speed up.

accented beat   a stressed pulse, creating strong and weak recurring patterns in meter.

accidentals   a sharp, flat, or natural which occurs outside the given key signature.

adagio   a slow tempo but not as slow as Largo.

agitato   agitated.

allegretto   fast and lively but not as much as allegro. Literally, "a little less allegro."

allegro   fast and lively.

anacrusis   a pick-up beat (or beats) before the first downbeat.

andante   a slow, walking tempo.

andantino   a little faster than andante.

animato   animated.

antecedent   the question phrase in a period.

antiphonal   describing two musical groups which perform alternately in call-response.

appassionato   passionately.

aria   solo song in opera, oratorio, or cantata which is usually accompanied by an orchestra.

arpeggio   a broken chord in which tones are heard successively.

assai   modifying adverb meaning "very." *Assai allegro* means very quick.

asymmetrical meter   a non-symmetrical meter such as five, seven, etc.

a tempo   return to the original tempo.

augmented interval   an interval that is a half-step larger than perfect (in the case of unisons, fourths, fifths, and octaves) or a half-step larger than major (in the case of seconds, thirds, sixths, and sevenths). C to F♯ is an augmented fourth.

bar line   dividing line between measures.

bass clef   F clef, which indicates the placement of F below middle C.

beam   straight line flags that join notes (eighths or smaller).

beat   single pulse of the basic duration. Usually a quarter, half, or eighth note, sometimes a dotted quarter.

binary form   two-part form, whether AB or AA_1.

brass   instruments made of metal with cup–or funnel–shaped mouthpieces, including trumpet, French horn, trombone, and tuba.

cadence   a resting point in music, usually at the end of a phrase.

calypso   music of Trinidad characterized by syncopated rhythm and satirical lyrics.

canon   a piece in which each part starts at a different time yet has the same (or a similar) melody.

cantabile   in a singing style.

capo   a device placed across the neck of a guitar to raise the pitch of all strings uniformly.

changing meter meters which change every measure.

chord several pitches played simultaneously as a unit.

chromatic a twelve-toned scale with a half-step between adjacent tones, i.e. C C♯ D D♯ E F F♯ G G♯ A A♯ B C′

circle of fifths arrangement of all major/minor keys to show progression of sharp and flat keys.

coda ending of a piece.

complete cadence a resting point which sounds finished. It usually ends on the I chord.

compound interval an interval greater than an octave.

con brio with vigor and spirit.

conducting patterns

conjunct stepwise motion.

con moto with movement.

consequent the answer phrase in a period.

contour melodic direction.

contrast change; variety.

couplet two rhyming lines of poetry.

crescendo to become louder gradually.

Curwen hand signals a system in which each syllable of the scale is represented by a specific hand shape.

D.C. al Fine da capo al Fine—return to the "head" or beginning of the music and play to the "finish" or Fine.

decrescendo or **diminuendo** to become softer gradually.

definite pitch percussion instruments in which distinct pitches are played, especially those keyboard instruments played with mallets.

descant a second melody that is performed above the main melody; higher countermelody.

disjunct skipwise motion.

dolce sweetly.

dominant the fifth note of the major or minor scale (*sol* or *mi,* respectively) as well as the triad built on that note.

dominant seventh triad built on the fifth note of the scale with an added seventh.

dorian mode a diatonic scale in pattern of 1 ½ 1 1 1 ½ 1, i.e. d e f g a b c d′.

dot a device (·) to lengthen the duration of a note by one-half its original value.

dotted quarter note ♩. a note that is half again as long as a ♩
If ♩ = 1, ♩. = 1½.

If ♩ = 2, ♩. = 3.

dotted quarter rest ♩. the rest equivalent to a dotted quarter note.

double bar two bar lines used to signal the end of a song or section.

double reed woodwind instrument in which performer blows between two pieces of cane. Oboe and bassoon are both double reed instruments.

D.S. al Fine repeat from the sign 𝄋 and play to the finish (Fine).

duet a piece for two performers or parts.

duplet two notes in the time of three.

duple time strong-weak meters. ²⁄₄ ²⁄₂ ¢ ²⁄₈ ⁶⁄₈

dynamic markings using forte (*f*) and piano (*p*) with modifications to indicate relative degree of loudness.

dynamics loudness of music.

echo song one song performed in two parts as call-response.

eighth note ♪ one half of a quarter note.

eighth rest ⁊ rest equivalent of an eighth note.

enharmonic pitches or chords that sound alike but are written differently, i.e. C♯ and D♭.

espressivo expressively.

even pattern rhythm pattern in which every note moves exactly with the pulse or is divided evenly over the pulse.

fermata ⌒ A hold.

fifth the third note in a triad. In the C major triad (C E G), G is the fifth.

first, second endings a device for repeating a section of a piece in which different endings are used with each repetition.

flag the appendage on an eighth note ♪ that distinguishes it from a quarter. Sixteenth notes have two flags ♬, thirty-second notes, three ♬, and so on.

flat (♭) a symbol that lowers a tone by one-half step.

folk song a simple song of a national group.

form musical design.

grand staff joining the treble and bass staff to create a continuous range of pitches.

grave slow and solemn.

grazioso gracefully.

half note 𝅗𝅥 One half of a whole note or twice the duration of a quarter note.

half rest ▬ rest equivalent of a half note.

harmonic minor a diatonic scale built on *la* with *sol* (7) raised one-half step to *si*.

harmony sounding at the same time of two or more different pitches.

heptatonic seven-toned scale

homophony texture with melody and accompaniment.

improvisation creating a new melody or elaborating on an old one impromptu.

incomplete cadence a resting point that sounds unfinished. It usually ends on a chord *other* than the tonic.

indefinite pitch percussion instruments in which distinct pitches are not discerned, i.e. snare drum, bass drum, cymbals, etc.

interlude musical filler between main ideas.

interval distance between two pitches.

introduction music which comes before the main idea or section.

inversion a chord whose root is not the lowest sounding tone; a rearrangement of the pitches from root position.

keynote first tone of a scale—*do* in major, *la* in minor.

key signature a group of sharps or flats at the beginning of each staff of music to indicate the key.

largo very slow.

legato smooth and flowing.

leger line a short line added to indicate a note above or below the regular staff.

lydian mode a diatonic scale in pattern of 1 1 1 ½ 1 1 ½, i.e. f g a b c d e f′.

maestoso majestically.

major diatonic a scale in the pattern of 1 1 ½ 1 1 1 ½, i.e. c d e f g a b c′.

major interval refers to seconds, thirds, sixths, and sevenths and their compoound equivalents. Half-step larger than a minor interval.

    C to D ____ major second   C to A ____ major sixth
    C to E ____ major third   C to B ____ major seventh

measure (bar) rhythmic unit determined by meter and separated by bar lines. In $\frac{4}{4}$, a measure is equivalent to four quarter notes.

melodic minor a diatonic scale built on *la* with *fa* (6) and *sol* (7) raised one-half step ascending to *fi* and *si*, respectively, but returned to the original tones (same as natural minor scale) descending.

melodic rhythm the rhythm of the words.

melody a series of pitches that are heard as a unit.

meno   less.

meter signature   written indication of strong-weak (etc.) pulses.

metronome   a device that sounds (or displays) a steady pulse. It may be set to slow and fast tempos.

minor interval   an interval one-half step smaller than a major. Only seconds, thirds, sixths, and sevenths and their compound equivalents may be minor.

C to D♭ _____ minor second   C to A♭ _____ minor sixth
C to E♭ _____ minor third   C to B♭ _____ minor seventh

mixolydian mode   a diatonic scale in pattern of 1 1 ½ 1 1 ½ 1, i.e. g a b c d e f g′.

mode   a diatonic scale.

moderato   moderately.

modulation   changing from one key to another within a composition.

molto   very; much.

monophony   single line of melody without accompaniment.

mosso   motion.

motive   a short rhythmic or melodic (sometimes harmonic) pattern.

natural (♮)   a symbol that cancels out a sharp or flat.

natural minor   a diatonic scale built on *la*.

non-harmonic tone   a pitch that is outside a given chord.

non troppo   not too much.

octave   an interval of eight pitch names, i.e. c to c′.

opera   staged drama that is predominantly sung, with orchestral accompaniment.

ostinato   a repeated pattern, whether in rhythm, melody or harmony.

overture   an extended orchestral introduction to an opera or ballet or similar type of musical work.

parallel keys   tonalities that have the same keynote but different key signatures, i.e. C major and c minor.

partner songs   two songs that have identical harmony and which can be performed together. This may sometimes include the verse and chorus of the same song.

passing tone   a non-harmonic tone that passes between harmonic tones. If the harmony is C E G, then D and F would be passing tones.

patschen   slap on the thigh.

pentatonic   a five-tone scale, most commonly, *do re mi sol la*.

percussion   instruments that are struck, shaken, or scraped.

perfect interval   an interval of perfect consonance. It may be unison, fourth, fifth, and octave (or compounds) only.

period   a two-phrase structure consisting of antecedent and consequent.

phrase   a "breath" length in the melody; a melodic unit ending with a cadence.

phrygian mode   a diatonic scale in pattern of ½ 1 1 1 ½ 1 1, i.e. e f g a b c d e′.

più   more.

pizzicato   plucked strings.

poco   little.

polyphony   texture with two or more melodies simultaneously.

polyrhythm   two or more rhythms simultaneously, with different accents or meters; cross-rhythm.

prestissimo   faster than presto.

presto   faster than allegro.

primary triad   tonic, subdominant, or dominant triad.

program music   music which has an extra-musical reference, such as a narrative or description.

quadruple time (⁴₄ ⁴₂ ⁴₈ ¹²₈ C)   strong-weak-weak-weak meters.

quarter note ♩   one half of a half note.

quarter rest 𝄽   rest equivalent of a quarter note.

quartet   a piece for four performers or parts.

range   interval between the highest and lowest pitches.

refrain   a chorus of music repeated at intervals in a song, especially following each verse.

relative keys   tonalities that have the same key signatures but different keynotes, i.e. C major and a minor.

repetition   repeating of melody, rhythm, or harmony, generally to create musical unity.

rhythm   temporal element of music including tempo, beat, meter, and pattern, whether even, uneven, or syncopated.

ritardando   a gradual slowing of the tempo.

rondo   a return form in lively tempo. Common designs are ABA, ABABA, ABACA, and ABACABA.

root   the tone upon which a chord is based.

root position   a chord with the root as the lowest sounding pitch.

round   a strict canon.

SATB   abbreviation for soprano, alto, tenor, and bass.

secondary dominant   a dominant seventh built on tones other than the dominant, especially the supertonic, mediant, submediant, but also the tonic or subdominant.

secondary triad   triad built on the supertonic, mediant, or submediant.

sempre   always

sequence   repetition of a melodic idea at a higher or lower pitch.

sharp (♯)   a symbol that raises a tone by one-half step.

simple interval   an interval that is less than an octave.

single reed   a woodwind instrument in which the performer blows through a mouthpiece equipped with one piece of cane. Clarinet and saxophone are single reed instruments.

sixteenth note ♬   a note equal to one-half the duration of an eighth note.

sixteenth rest ♪   rest equivalent of a sixteenth note.

slur   a curved line ⌣ between two or more notes of different pitch names indicating they are to be played legato.

sostenuto   sustained.

staccato   detached; short.

staff notation   placement of notes on five lines and four spaces.

stem   black vertical line attached to all notes except the whole note. ♩ ♩ ♪

string instruments   instruments producing sound by taut strings that are bowed or plucked; violin, viola, cello, and double bass, but also guitar and harp.

strophic   exact repetition.

subdominant   fourth tone of the major or minor scale (*fa* or *re,* respectively); a triad built on this is called the subdominant triad, IV (iv).

supertonic   the second tone of a scale.

syllables   *do re mi fa sol la ti do'.*

syncopation   shifting a strong beat to a weak one or leaving it out.

ternary form   three-part form, most commonly ABA.

theme and variations   presentation of a theme and then several transformations of it.

third   the second note in a triad. In the C major triad (C E G), E is the third.

tie   a connecting line ⌣ between two or more notes of the same pitch for lengthening the first by the duration of the following one(s).

timbre   tone color of sound.

tonic   the first note of the major or minor scale, *do* or *la,* respectively.

transposition   to play, write or read a song in a different key than its original.

treble clef   G clef, which indicates the placement of G above middle C. 𝄞

triad   a chord of three tones, each separated by the interval of a third.

trio   a piece for three performers or parts.

triplet   three notes in the time of two. ♫♩ = ♫

triple time ³⁄₄ ³⁄₂ ³⁄₈ ⁹⁄₈   strong-weak-weak meters.

uneven pattern   rhythm pattern in which notes do not move exactly with the pulse.

unity repetition.

variety contrast.

verse a stanza of music used with new words before each refrain.

whole note o a note equal to two half notes or four quarters.

whole rest ⌐ rest equivalent of a whole note.

whole-tone scale a six-tone scale with a whole-step between adjacent tones, i.e. c d e f♯ g♯ a♯ c′.

woodwinds instruments in which tone is produced by a vibrating air column inside a pipe. The pipe is equipped with finger holes. Includes flute, oboe, clarinet, bassoon.

Chapter Review Answer Key

Chapter 1

1. harmony
2. variety
3. unity
4. program
5. melody
6. form
7. folk
8. chord
9. timbre
10. rhythm
11. sound
12. flute
13. six
14. tune

Chapter 2

1. L
2. I
3. U
4. O
5. D
6. P
7. F
8. R
9. G
10. J
11. H
12. A
13. M
14. E
15. Q
16. C
17. S
18. K
19. B
20. N
21. T

Chapter 3

1. ⌒
2. metronome
3. accelerando
4. ritardando
5. aria
6. (chord diagram)
7. (chord diagram)
8. A
9. C♯
10. F♯
11. G
12. D
13. A
14. G
15. B
16. improvise
17. largo
18. adagio
19. grave
20. andante
21. E
22. B
23. C
24. I
25. D
26. A
27. F
28. J
29. H
30. G

Chapter 4

1. $\frac{2}{4}$
2. $\frac{3}{8}$
3. $\frac{4}{2}$
4. $\frac{3}{4}$
5. $\frac{9}{8}$ or $\frac{3}{♩.}$
6. $\frac{6}{8}$ or $\frac{2}{♩.}$
7. $\frac{2}{2}$ or ¢
8. $\frac{4}{4}$ or C
9. $\frac{4}{8}$
10. $\frac{12}{8}$ or $\frac{4}{♩.}$

Matching

A.	7	G.	6	M.	5
B.	1	H.	4	N.	3
C.	9	I.	14	O.	10
D.	12	J.	17	P.	11
E.	16 (possibly 3)	K.	15	Q.	8
F.	2	L.	13		

Chapter 5

1.	C	6.	D	11.	L
2.	B	7.	G	12.	O
3.	A	8.	I	13.	M
4.	J	9.	F	14.	K
5.	E	10.	H	15.	N

Matching

1.	B	9.	U	17.	P
2.	D	10.	I	18.	J
3.	F	11.	X	19.	O
4.	C	12.	K	20.	S
5.	R	13.	Y	21.	W
6.	E	14.	G	22.	L
7.	N	15.	M	23.	T
8.	A	16.	V	24.	H
				25.	Q

Chapter 6

1.	K	8.	R	15.	N
2.	M	9.	T	16.	F
3.	Q	10.	L	17.	G
4.	H	11.	J	18.	S
5.	C	12.	D	19.	P
6.	A	13.	O	20.	E
7.	B	14.	I		

Chapter 7

1.	H	8.	D	15.	M
2.	J	9.	B	16.	Q
3.	E	10.	C	17.	S
4.	F	11.	A	18.	P
5.	K	12.	R	19.	L
6.	I	13.	N	20.	O
7.	G	14.	T		

Crossword Puzzle

	Across		Down
1.	syncopated	2.	couplet
3.	A	4.	cow
4.	chord	7.	E
5.	*loo*	8.	guiro
6.	uneven	9.	*mf*
10.	ff	10.	*f*
11.	flat	11.	F
13.	*la*	12.	ten(th)
14.	*do*		
15.	even		
16.	or		
17.	-junct		
18.	solo		

Chapter 8

1.	D	6.	A♭	11.	B₇
2.	G	7.	C	12.	A major
3.	E♭	8.	F♮	13.	E major
4.	C♯	9.	C♭	14.	key of E major
5.	F♯	10.	G♭		

Word Find

1.	mezzo forte	6.	cadence	11.	clef
2.	mezzo piano	7.	phrase	12.	grand
3.	fortissimo	8.	question	13.	triplet
4.	pianissimo	9.	answer	14.	period
5.	rondo	10.	crescendo	15.	coda
				16.	duplet

Chapter 9

Crossword Puzzle

	Across		Down
1.	pentatonic	1.	*pp*
6.	*sol*	2.	echo
7.	*mi*	3.	two
8.	A	4.	ostinato
9.	-phonal	5.	*la*
11.	variation	6.	*sol*
13.	*pp*	9.	*p*
15.	*do*	10.	and
		12.	*re*
		13.	*p*

Chapter 10

1.	5th	8.	12th	15.	augmented 4th
2.	4th	9.	8va	16.	perfect 5th
3.	8va	10.	unison	17.	major 6th
4.	2nd	11.	6, 8	18.	minor 6th
5.	6th	12.	major 3rd	19.	major 7th
6.	11th	13.	minor 3rd	20.	minor 7th
7.	5th	14.	perfect 4th	21.	perfect 5th

Matching

1.	G	6.	O	11.	E
2.	C	7.	H	12.	I
3.	J	8.	P	13.	L
4.	M	9.	A	14.	N
5.	B	10.	K	15.	D
				16.	F

Chapter 11

1.	W	13.	B	25.	E♭
2.	J	14.	A	26.	B
3.	R	15.	C	27.	B♭
4.	T	16.	S	28.	A
5.	K	17.	Q	29.	A♭
6.	N	18.	L	30.	G
7.	H	19.	P	31.	E
8.	O	20.	E	32.	C
9.	U	21.	G	33.	F
10.	I	22.	F	34.	F♯
11.	V	23.	M	35.	D♭
12.	D	24.	D	36.	G♭

Chapter 12

1.	K	11.	M	21.	B♮
2.	F	12.	L	22.	C♯
3.	C	13.	J	23.	E♮
4.	I	14.	O	24.	D♯
5.	A	15.	R	25.	F♯, G♯
6.	E	16.	N	26.	E♮, F♯
7.	H	17.	Q	27.	A♮, B♮
8.	D	18.	P	28.	B♮, C♯
9.	B	19.	G♯	29.	D♮, E♮
10	G	20.	F♯	30.	C♯, D♯

Chapter 13

Matching

1.	H	8.	O	15.	L
2.	N	9.	F	16.	M
3.	V	10.	U	17.	S
4.	K	11.	R	18.	B
5.	C	12.	I	19.	D
6.	Q	13.	A	20.	G
7.	E	14.	T	21.	P
				22.	J

Chapter 14

Matching

1.	C	4.	D	7.	A
2.	G	5.	J	8.	E
3.	I	6.	F	9.	H
				10.	B

Baroque (English) fingering for soprano recorder in C

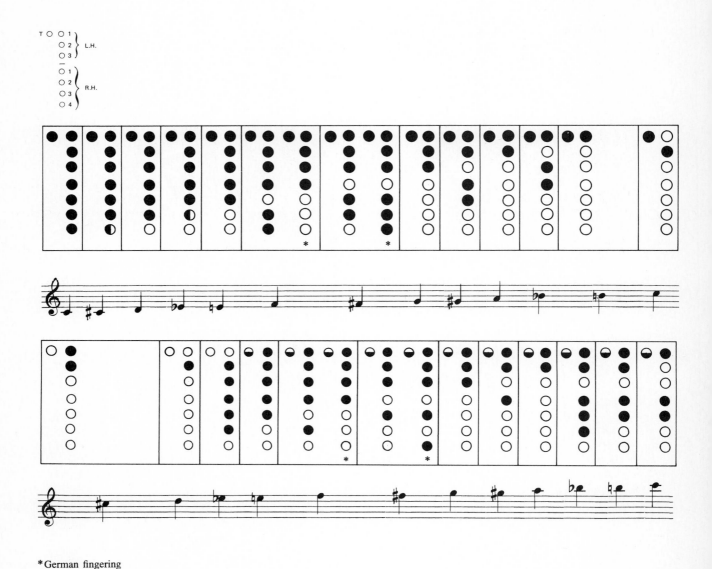

*German fingering

Guitar Tuning

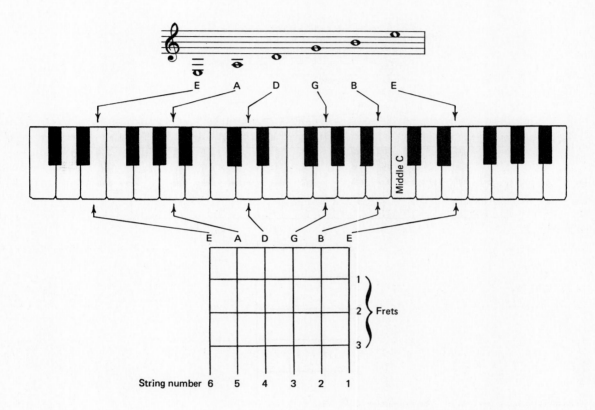

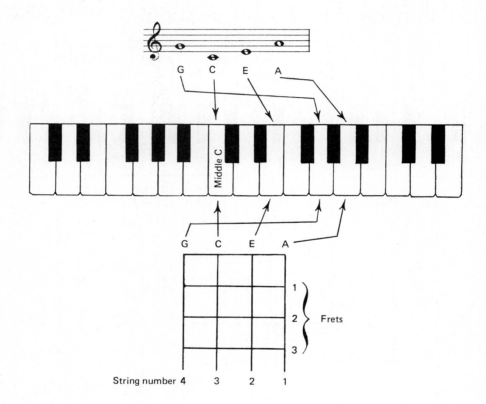

Fifteen Bar Autoharp Chart

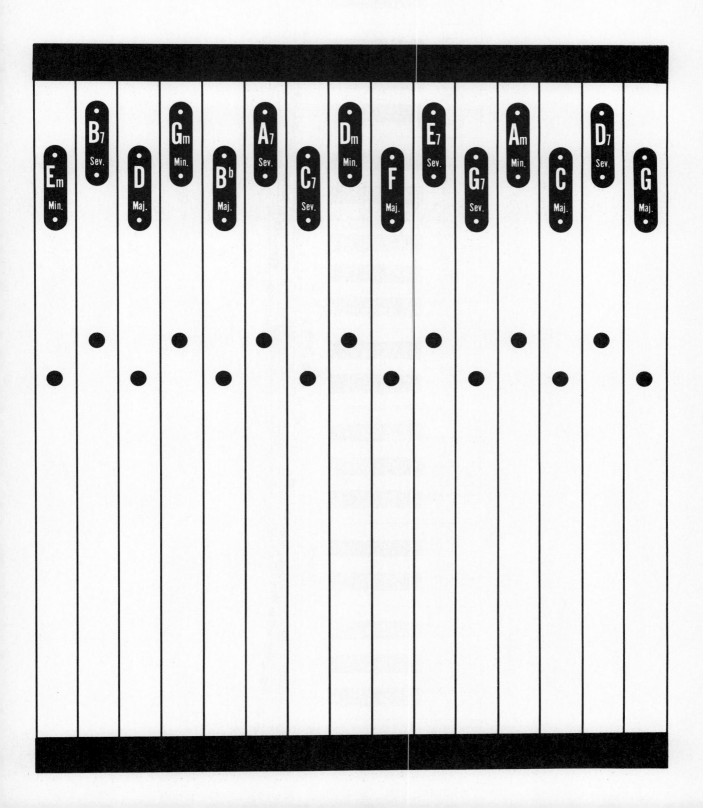

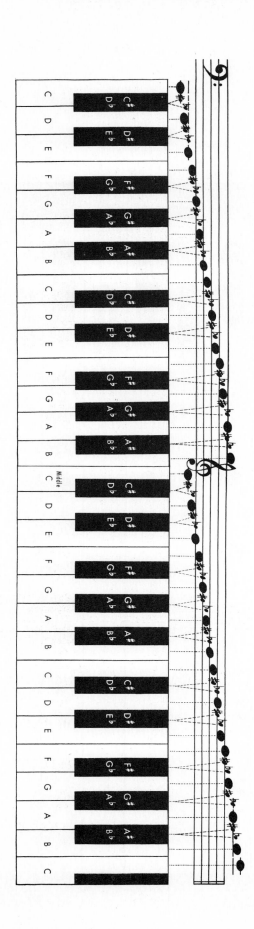

Common Guitar, Ukulele, and Piano Chords

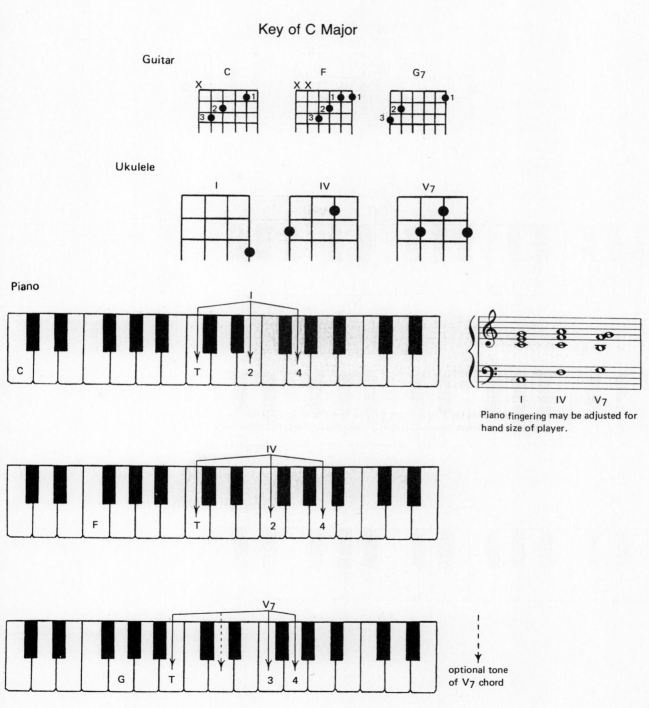

Key of C Major

Guitar

Ukulele

Piano

Piano fingering may be adjusted for hand size of player.

optional tone of V₇ chord

Key of a Minor

Guitar

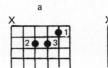

Ukulele

Piano

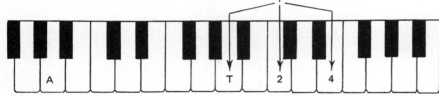

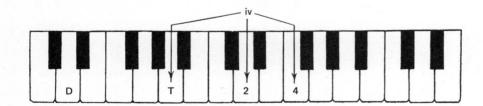

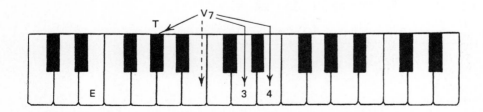

Key of G Major

Guitar

G

C

D7

Ukulele

I

IV

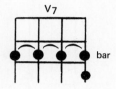
V7

Piano

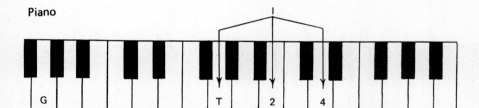

I   IV   V7

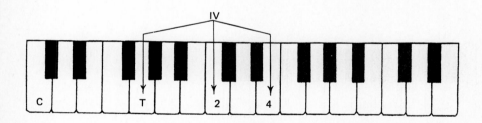

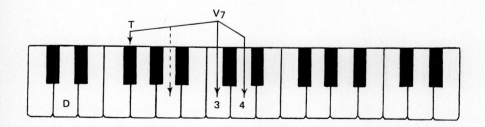

Key of e Minor

Guitar

Ukulele

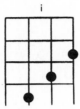

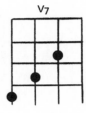

Piano

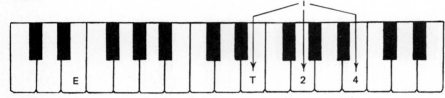

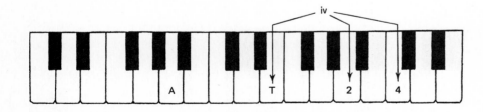

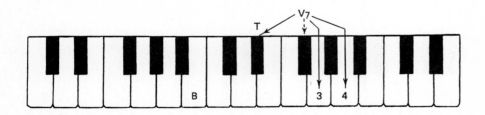

Key of F Major

Guitar

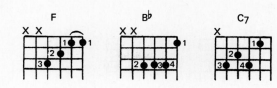

Ukulele

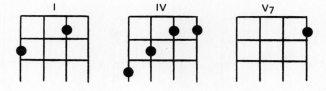

Piano

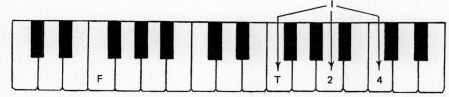

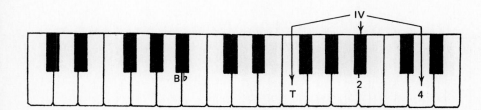

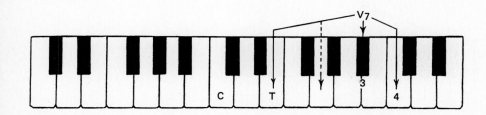

Key of d,Minor

Guitar

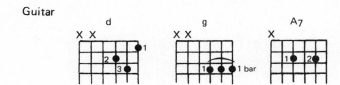

Ukulele

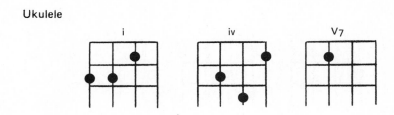

Piano

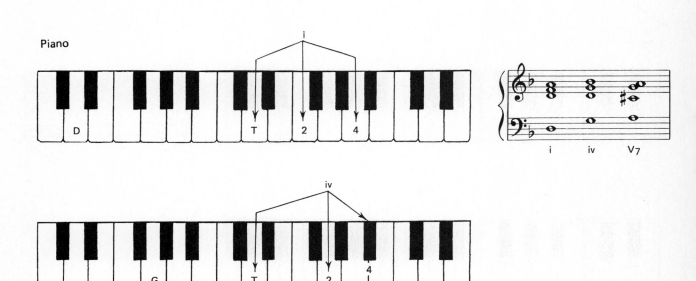

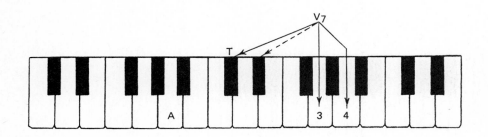

Key of D Major

Guitar

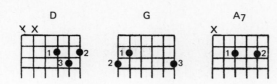

Ukulele

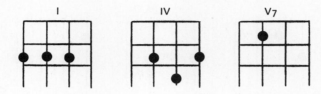

Piano

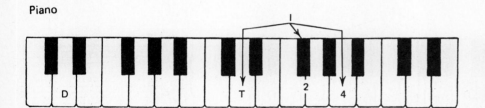

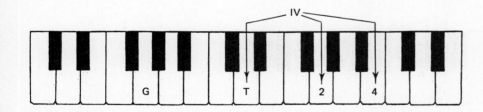

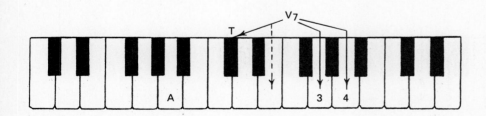

Key of A Major

Guitar

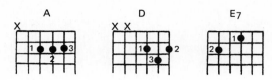

Ukulele

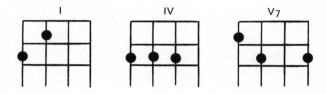

Piano

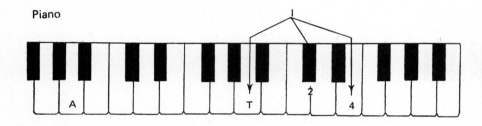

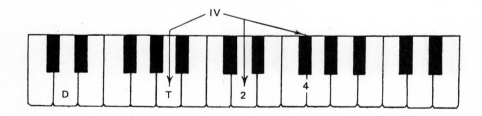

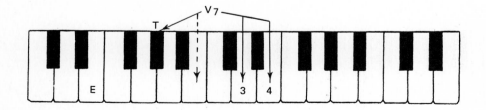

Key of B♭ Major

Guitar

Place capo on first fret
and read as if A major.

B♭   E♭   F₇

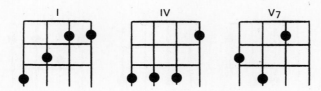

Ukulele

I   IV   V₇

Piano

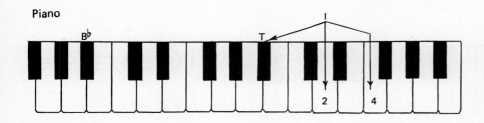

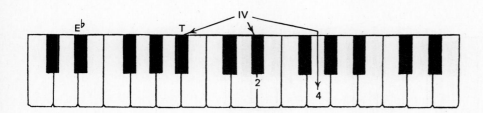

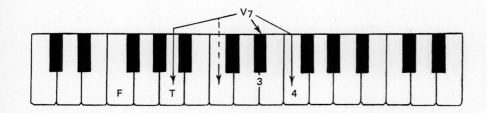

Key of E♭ Major

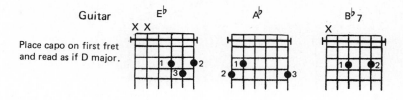

Guitar

Place capo on first fret and read as if D major.

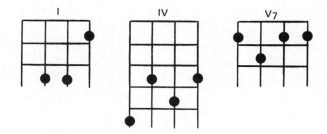

Ukulele

Piano

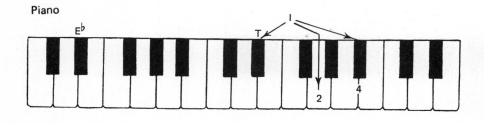

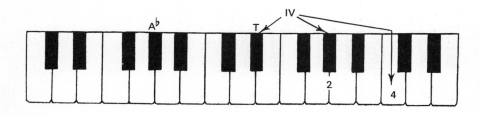

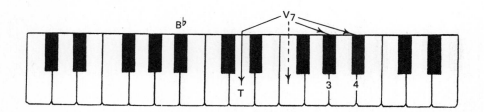

226

Key of A♭ Major

Guitar

Place capo on first fret and read as if G major.

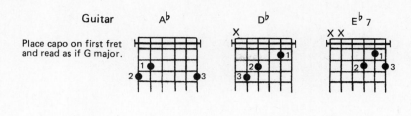

A♭   D♭   E♭7

Ukulele

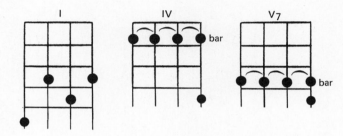

I   IV   V7

Piano

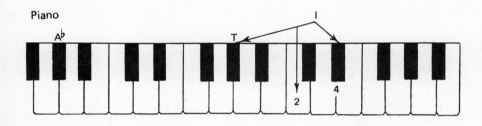

I   IV   V7

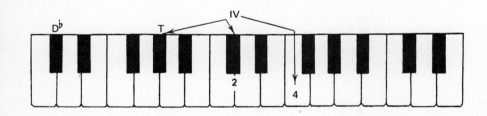

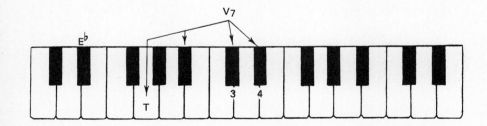

Musical Skills and Activities

Chapter 1

Singing

She'll be Comin' Round the Mountain
The Caissons Go Rolling Along
Polly Wolly Doodle
Home on the Range
Star Spangled Banner

Listening

The Moldau (Smetana)

Chapter 2

Singing

Are you Sleeping?
Hey, Ho! Nobody Home
Lovely Evening
Row, Row, Row Your Boat

Listening

The March of the Siamese Children (Rodgers)
Stars and Stripes Forever (Sousa)
Colonel Bogey March (Alford)

Playing

Guitar/Autoharp

D major
e minor

Classroom Percussion

woodblock
sticks
drum
guiro

Creating

duets
trios
quartets
introductions
codas

Moving

tap
clap
snap
patschen
walk

Chapter 3

Singing

Beside Thy Cradle
Bye'm Bye
Wayfaring Stranger
Go Tell Aunt Rhodie
Jacob's Ladder

Listening

Overture to "The Bat" (Strauss)
Carnival of the Animals (Saint–Saens)
In the Hall of the Mountain King (Grieg)
Hungarian Dance No. 5 (Brahms)

Playing

Guitar/Autoharp	*Classroom Percussion*	*Recorder*	*Piano*
a minor	triangle		D major
A₇	tambourine	g a b	A₇

Creating

chord patterns
melodies with g, a, b

Chapter 4

Singing

Billy Boy
The Bus Song
Sandy Land
A Bell Noël
Scotland's Burning
Row, Row, Row Your Boat
We're All Together Again
Join Into the Game
The Man on the Flying Trapeze
The Upward Trail

Listening

March Militaire (Schubert)
Dance of the Sugar Plum Fairy (Tchaikovsky)
Trepak (Tchaikovsky)
Arabian Dance (Tchaikovsky)
On the Trail (Grofe)
Skater's Waltzes (Waldteufel)
Grand Waltz (Lecocq)
Waltz of the Flowers (Tchaikovsky)
Jesu, Joy of Man's Desiring (Bach)
Royal March of the Lion (Saint-Saens)
March of the Dwarfs (Grieg)
Minuet (Mozart)
Triumphal March (Verdi)
Gypsy Rondo (Haydn)
Sleeping Beauty Waltz (Tchaikovsky)

Playing

Guitar/Autoharp	*Classroom Percussion*	*Recorder*	*Piano*
G major	bongo		G major
D₇	conga	d c♯ c f♯	D₇
C major	claves		C major
	maracas		

Creating

melodies with five tones
descants

Chapter 5

Singing

For Health and Strength
Puffer Billies
Clocks and Watches
This Old Man
St. Paul's Steeple
Magic Bell Song
See the Little Ducklings
Jim Along, Josie
Good King Wenceslas
Old MacDonald Had a Farm
Eins, Zwei, Drei

Six Little Ducks
Niño Querido
Come Rowing With Me
East Side, West Side
Old Roger is Dead
Beautiful Apples
Chiapanecas
Sleep, Baby, Sleep!

Listening

Sleeping Beauty Waltz (Tchaikovsky)

Playing

Guitar/Autoharp	*Classroom Percussion*	*Recorder*	*Piano*
F major	song bells		F major
D_7, G_7	resonator bells		C_7
	stepbells		C major
			G_7

d e f c b♭

Noël
Melody (Brahms)
Au Clair de la Lune
Canon

Creating

even patterns
ostinatos
adding words to songs
descants

Moving

conducting meter in 2,3,4

Chapter 6

Singing

Die Musici
America
We Gather Together
America, the Beautiful
Christmas is Coming
My White Mouse
Alouette

The Railroad Train
Here We Come A-Wassailing
Rig-A-Jig-Jig

Listening

Third movement/Third Symphony (Brahms)

Playing

Guitar/Autoharp	*Classroom Percussion*	*Recorder*	*Piano*
pick-strum	jingle clogs		root-chord
G,C,D_7	sand blocks		G,C,D_7
F,C_7	handle castanets		F,C_7
	finger castanets		

high e g♯ c♯

Theme-Finlandia
Summer is A-Coming In

Creating

uneven patterns
recorder patterns

Chapter 7

Singing

Vesper Hymn
Mein Hut
My Lord, What a Morning
Nobody Knows the Trouble I've Seen
Riding in the Buggy
Time for Work
Persian Rhythm
John the Rabbit
Caught a Rabbit
Old House
Tinga Layo

Hey Lidee
Round the Bay of Mexico
Rock Island Line
Joshua Fought the Battle
The First Noel

Listening

Golliwog's Cakewalk (Debussy)
Infernal Dance of Koschai (Stravinsky)
Funeral March of a Marionette (Gounod)

Playing

Guitar/Autoharp	*Classroom Percussion*	*Recorder*	*Piano*
C,F,G$_7$	cowbell		root-chord C, F, G$_7$
a,E$_7$	xylophone		F, B♭, C$_7$
chromatic scale	metallophone		a, E$_7$
tuning (Autoharp)			chromatic scale
			melody ostinato

Creating

syncopated patterns
rewrite songs to include syncopation
calypso patterns

Chapter 8

Singing

The More We Get Together
Three Dukes
Patsy
Little Bird on My Window
The Muffin Man
White Coral Bells
Jig Along Home

One More River
Simple Gifts
The Linden Tree

Listening

The Sea and Sinbad's Ship (Rimsky–Korsakoff)

Playing

Guitar/Autoharp	*Piano*
E, A, B$_7$	E, A, B$_7$
	Root-chord in all keys so far

Creating

rondos
antecedent-consequent phrases
rounds with dynamic markings

Chapter 9

Singing

It's Raining
Sail, Silver Moon Boat
Hear the Echo
Before Dinner
Four in a Boat
All Night, All Day
One of these Days

Mr. Rabbit
Turn the Glasses Over
Mary Had a Baby
Swing Low, Sweet Chariot

Listening

Surprise Symphony (Haydn)

Playing

Guitar/Autoharp

pentatonic ostinatos

Recorder

high g

theme and variations

Piano

pentatonic ostinatos

Creating

rhythms with syllables
pentatonic duets
words to songs
variations on a theme
pentatonic ostinatos
partner songs

Chapter 10

Singing

Listen While My Flute is Playing
Make New Friends
Dona Nobis Pacem
All Through the Night
Drum and Fiddle
German Instrument Song
The Orchestra
We are Good Musicians

Listening

On the Steppes of Central Asia (Borodin)
Minuet (Mozart)
Young Person's Guide to the Orchestra (Britten)

Playing

Guitar/Autoharp

arpeggios

Piano

arpeggios

Creating

intervals
arpeggio accompaniments

Chapter 11

Singing

Chester
Lullaby
Kum Ba Yah
Michael, Row the Boat Ashore
Shuckin' of the Corn
An April Day
My Pony
East Side, West Side
The Wabash Cannon Ball
This Land is Your Land
Sweet Betsy from Pike
Pease Porridge Hot
J'ai Perdu Le Do

I Saw Three Ships
My Farm
Pussy Cat, Pussy Cat
Oh, Give Thanks
The Muffin Man
Now Thank We All Our God
O Come, Little Children

Listening

"Chester" from New England Triptych (Schuman)

Playing

Guitar/Autoharp

all major chords with capo

Recorder

high g♯   a   a♯   b

Piano

all major chords

Creating

melodies with diatonic scales
harmonizing melodies with I, IV and V_7

Chapter 12

Singing

Go Down, Moses
March of the Three Kings
All the Pretty Little Horses
Shalom Chaverim
The Ghost of John
Winter Holiday
God Rest You Merry Gentlemen

On Halloween
Candles of Hanukah

The Tailor and the Mouse
Lully, Lullay
Poor Mister Wind
Eight Nights of Hanukah
Dreydl Spin

Listening

Danse Macabre (Saint–Saens)

Playing

Guitar/Autoharp

all minor chords

Piano

all minor chords

Creating

melodies in minor
minor scales

Chapter 13

Singing

Drink to me Only with Thine Eyes	Bird's Courting Song
Marching to Pretoria	Halloween Sounds
Pop Goes the Weasel	
Who Did?	
Sing Your Way Home	
Old House	

Listening

"March to the Scaffold"
from Symphonie Fantastique (Berlioz)

Playing

Guitar/Autoharp	*Piano*
transposing chords	transposing chords

Creating

transposing melodies and improvisations

Chapter 14

Singing

When Johnny Comes Marching Home	Sabbath Evening
I'm a Yankee Doodle Dandy	Gerakina
Give My Regards to Broadway	
Meet Me in St. Louis, Louis	
Hawaiian Rainbows	
Changing of the Guard	

Listening

American Salute (Gould)

Playing

Recorder

When the Saints Go Marching In

Creating

melodies in the modes and whole-tone scale
asymmetric patterns
changing meters
polyrhythms

Song Index

Gerakina	F major	$\frac{7}{8}$	195–96
German Instrument Song	D major	$\frac{2}{4}$	134
Ghost of John, The	e minor	$\frac{4}{4}$	166
Give My Regards to Broadway	B♭ major	$\frac{4}{4}$	191
Go Down, Moses	a minor	$\frac{4}{4}$	161
God Rest You Merry, Gentlemen	e minor	$\frac{4}{4}$	166
Good King Wenceslas	G major	$\frac{4}{4}$	53
Go Tell Aunt Rhodie	D major	$\frac{2}{4}$	22
Halloween Sounds	D major	$\frac{6}{8}$	186
Hawaiian Rainbows	G major	$\frac{2}{2}$	191–92
Hear the Echo	C pentatonic	$\frac{2}{4}$	117, 118–19
Here We Come A-Wassailing	D major	$\frac{6}{8}/\frac{2}{2}$	79–80
Hey, Ho! Nobody Home	e minor	$\frac{2}{4}$	11–12
Hey Lidee	C major	$\frac{4}{4}$	94
Home on the Range	F major	$\frac{6}{8}$	3
I'm a Yankee Doodle Dandy	G major	$\frac{2}{4}$	190
I Saw Three Ships	F major	$\frac{6}{8}$	154
It's Raining	C pentatonic	$\frac{4}{4}$	116
Jacob's Ladder	D major	$\frac{2}{2}$	22–23
J'ai Perdu Le Do	F major	$\frac{2}{4}$	153
Jig Along Home	F major	$\frac{2}{4}$	109
Jim Along, Josie	C major	$\frac{4}{4}$	52
John the Rabbit	e minor	$\frac{2}{4}$	90
Join Into the Game	D major	$\frac{3}{4}$	38–40
Joshua Fought the Battle	a minor	$\frac{4}{4}$	98
Kum Ba Yah	C major	$\frac{4}{4}$	143
Linden Tree, The	E major	$\frac{3}{4}$	112
Listen While My Flute Is Playing	C major	$\frac{4}{4}$	127
Little Bird on My Window	F major	$\frac{3}{4}$	106
Lovely Evening	D major	$\frac{3}{2}$	14
Lullaby	C major	$\frac{4}{4}$	142
Lully, Lullay	g minor	$\frac{3}{4}$	169
Magic Bell Song	C major	$\frac{4}{4}$	52
Make New Friends	F major	$\frac{4}{4}$	128
Man on the Flying Trapeze, The	G major	$\frac{3}{8}$	40–41
March of the Three Kings	a minor	$\frac{4}{4}$	162–63, 185–86
Marching to Pretoria	D major	$\frac{2}{2}$	176–78
Mary Had a Baby	F pentatonic	$\frac{2}{2}$	124
Meet Me in St. Louis, Louis	B♭ major	$\frac{3}{4}$	191
Mein Hut	C major	$\frac{3}{4}$	85
Melody (Brahms)	G major	$\frac{4}{4}$	54
Michael, Row the Boat Ashore	C major	$\frac{4}{4}$	144
More We Get Together, The	F major	$\frac{3}{4}$	103
Mr. Rabbit	F pentatonic	$\frac{2}{4}$	123
Muffin Man, The	G major/B♭ major	$\frac{4}{4}$	107, 156
My Farm	F major	$\frac{4}{4}$	154–55
My Lord, What a Morning	E♭ major	$\frac{4}{4}$	87
My Pony	G major	$\frac{2}{4}$	148
My White Mouse	F major	$\frac{4}{4}$	77
Niño Querido	F major	$\frac{3}{4}$	55–56
Nobody Knows the Trouble I've Seen	G major	$\frac{4}{4}$	88–89
Noël	G major	$\frac{2}{2}$	53
Now Thank We All Our God	E♭ major	$\frac{4}{4}$	157
O Come, Little Children	E♭ major	$\frac{2}{4}$	158
Oh, Give Thanks	B♭ major	$\frac{2}{2}$	155
Old House	g minor	$\frac{2}{4}$	92, 183–84
Old MacDonald Had a Farm	G major	$\frac{4}{4}$	53

Index for Listening Selections

Subject Index

41, 944

MT   O'Brien, James
7   Patrick.
.02
1985   Creative music
             fundamentals

DATE	BORROWER'S NAME	
9/5/85	P Grundler	